1495

# The Gesell Institute's Child from One to Six

# The Gesell Institute's Child from One to Six

*Evaluating the Behavior of the Preschool Child*

Louise Bates Ames, Ph.D., Clyde Gillespie, B.S., Jacqueline Haines, A.B., Frances L. Ilg, M.D.

HARPER & ROW, PUBLISHERS
NEW YORK, HAGERSTOWN,
SAN FRANCISCO, LONDON

*1817*

Dedicated to the memory of our colleagues:

Doctors Arnold Gesell, Catherine S. Amatruda,
and Helen Thompson

THE GESELL INSTITUTE'S CHILD FROM ONE TO SIX: EVALUATING THE BEHAVIOR OF THE PRE-
SCHOOL CHILD. Copyright © 1979 by the Gesell Institute of Human Development. All rights
reserved. Printed in the United States of America. No part of this book may be used or reproduced in any manner whatsoever without written permission except in the case of brief quota-
tions embodied in critical articles and reviews. For information address Harper & Row, Publishers, Inc., 10 East 53rd Street, New York, N.Y. 10022. Published simultaneously in
Canada by Fitzhenry & Whiteside Limited, Toronto.

*Designer: Eve Kirch*

Library of Congress Cataloging in Publication Data

Main entry under title:
The Gesell Institute's child from one to six.
   Includes bibliographical references and index.
   1. Child psychology. 2. Infant psychology.
I. Ames, Louise Bates. II. Gesell Institute of Child
Development, New Haven.
BF721.G53 1979      155.4'22      79–1795
ISBN 0–06–010087–7

83 10 9 8 7 6 5 4

# Contents

# List of Tables

# Preface

It was in 1940 that the staff of the Yale Clinic of Child Development, as a group, revised and presented its child behavior tests for the age levels 18 months through 6 years. This presentation covered four fields of behavior: Motor, Adaptive, Language, and Personal-Social.

Now, nearly forty years later, the present authors find virtually this same battery of tests to be highly effective. In fact, the several other batteries that have borrowed heavily from our own would further point to its effectiveness. The Gesell Developmental Tests or some similar derivative are widely used both in this country and abroad.

However, even the best of tests must one day be revised, sharpened up, improved. Dr. Arnold Gesell's tests for infants and preschoolers first appeared in 1928 under the title *Infancy and Human Growth* (30) and have undergone repeated revisions ever since.

Our original plan was once again to present a revision of an earlier work, but changes in approach made it more practical to provide here a replacement rather than a revision.

Time and experience have confirmed our basic premise—that behavior develops in a patterned and highly predictable way and can be evaluated by means of simple, basic test situations. However, in over nearly half a decade of clinical experience, we have added some new tests to our battery and have dropped others. The present volume presents an updated version of the original 1928 Gesell Preschool Tests.

Also as a somewhat theoretical exercise, it has been of interest to us, and we hope will be of interest to our readers, to determine to what extent young children of the 1970s develop and behave as did those of the 1930s. (It turns out that the similarities are substantial; the differences slight.)

Two of our original authors, Doctors Frances L. Ilg and Louise Bates Ames, with the cooperation of Dr. Janet Learned Rodell, had the privilege of founding the Gesell Institute of Child Development, which since 1950 has continued the work begun at the Yale Clinic of Child Development. With the help of colleagues, especially Clyde Gillespie and Jacqueline Haines, we have continued to use the basic test battery described in *The First Five Years of Life.* (Five of our original authors—Doctors Arnold Gesell, Helen Thompson, Catherine Amatruda, Henry Halverson, and Burton M. Castner—are no longer living.)

Thus we have at least to some extent continuity of authorship, of point of view, of instrument. As to point of view—our belief that behavior is to a large extent biologically determined and that it develops in a patterned, predictable, and measurable way has remained steadfast during a period when many behavioral scientists have practiced and preached a so-called "environmental mystique."

Our position, and our strong belief in the integrity of the organism, has sometimes been interpreted as meaning that we do not "believe in" or are not interested in the environment or in the *interaction* of organism and environment. Quite the contrary. Dr. Gesell, as early as 1940 (31), stated specifically:

> In appraising growth characteristics we must not ignore environmental influences. . . . But these must always be considered in relation to primary, or constitutional, factors because the latter ultimately determine the degree and even the mode of the reaction to the so-called environment. The organism always participates in the creation of its environment. And the growth characteristics of the child are really the end-product expressions of an *interaction* between intrinsic and extrinsic determiners. *Because the interaction is the crux, the distinction between these two sets of determiners should not be drawn too heavily.*

The fact that we are interested in measuring behavior normatively by no means implies that we stop there. In a clinical service, any diagnosis should be, and is, only the first step to treatment, treatment which in most instances involves manipulation of the environment.

A totally new aspect of the present volume is that we have based our findings on the behavior of an entirely new group of children.

Also in this investigation we have taken more care than in the past that our subjects should be representative of the entire gamut of socioeconomic levels. Though nearly all were Caucasians and all resided in the state of Connecticut, present subjects represent, in the proportion in which they appear in the U.S. Census figures for 1960, the following eleven categories: (1) professonal, technical, and kindred workers; (2) farmers and farm managers; (3) managers, officials, and proprietors; (4) clerical and kindred workers; (5) sales workers; (6) craftsmen, foremen, and kindred workers; (7) operatives and kindred workers; (8 and 9) service workers, including private household workers; (10) farm laborers and foremen; (11) laborers (except farm and mine).

Forty girls and forty boys were examined at each six-month age level from 2½ through 6 years of age, giving a total of 320 girls and 320 boys. Children whose ages fell between 2 years 4 months and 2 years 6 months were grouped as 2½-year-olds; those between 2 years 11 months and 3 years 1 month as 3-year-olds; and so on.

Subjects for *The First Five Years of Life,* with whom we compared present subjects, were actually not too different in manner of selection. The range of parental occupations was narrower, but the average subject probably stood at approximately the same place in the occupational scale. It was assumed, at that earlier date, that children of the middle 50% of the population would be correspondingly average. Parents, classified according to Florence Goodenough's Occupational Categories (36), were 90% in Groups III and IV (Group I being the highest occupational category listed and Group VI the lowest). One hundred % of the parents fell in Categories III, IV, and V.

Thus the *tests* described here are similar to those presented in the earlier book *The First Five Years of Life,* but they are not identical. The *subjects,* though in the same age range and of approximately the same socioeconomic status, are entirely different. Our *point of view* remains what it has always been—that human behavior develops in a patterned, highly predictable manner which can be measured and evaluated. This book will tell educators and psychologists how to examine preschoolers, and for parents it will describe general behavior characteristics and age changes which may be expected in the first six years of life.

# PART ONE

# 1

## Introduction

The Gesell philosophy of human behavior maintains, and has always maintained, that behavior is a function of structure. This means that to a large extent we behave as we do because of the way our bodies are built, and because of the stage of development we have reached.

Though our emphasis is, and always has been, on the body itself, as suggested in our preface, we have always been aware of and concerned with the interaction of body and environment. However, we have never agreed with those who maintain that one could make any child into anything he or she might wish. Actually, as time goes on our interpretation of environment shifts to some extent from other human beings to finer and more subtle aspects of the environment, such as those emphasized in orthomolecular medicine.

Those interested in orthomolecular medicine believe that thoughts, emotions, actions are strongly affected by the physical condition of the body, and that the nervous system cannot be expected to perform its complicated functions unless it is provided with the proper chemical milieu.

Our own increasing interest in this field, then, has led us to a special interest in environmental factors such as the food we eat, the fluids we drink, the very air we breathe. It is these aspects of environment with which we are currently concerned.

However, the present volume, though based on our assumption that behavior *is* a function of structure as it reacts to its physical as well as social environment, is devoted primarily to a study of behavior and not of structure. Its purpose is to describe, for parents, teachers, psychologists, and most especially for those who will be examining and evaluating the development of child behavior, those stages through which normal and measurable behaviors develop.

We have focused on behaviors which can be evaluated by means of simple test measures and situations, and have emphasized four special fields of behavior: motor, adaptive, language, and personal-social.

It has been our finding through the years, even as Dr. Arnold Gesell demonstrated in the early part of the century, that most human behaviors develop in a patterned way through largely predictable stages. Each individual will go through these stages at his own pace, but the sequence itself remains remarkably predictable.

Two of the outstanding laws or rules of development which may be of interest to readers are (1) the principle of cephalocaudad development and (2) the principle of reciprocal interweaving. According to the first, behavior in the human organism develops chiefly in a head-to-foot direction; that is, head and arms move effectively long before the lower trunk and legs. According to the second rule, in any growing behavior (or area of behavior), it is possible to identify paired-but-opposed types of response that occur in repeated alternation until the behavior has reached its final or complete stage, spiraling upward as it progresses.

Thus behavior does not simply develop in a straight-line direction, the immature gradually and without lapse giving way to the mature. Rather, if one of these opposites can be identified as immature and the other as mature (as is usually the case), we must anticipate repeated recurrences of the more immature behavior alternating with the more mature as the child grows older.

In such an area as prone progression, where the chief alternating behaviors are flexion and extension, the adult as a rule can view these alternations objectively. In such an area as handedness (where the responses alternating may be right-handedness, left-handedness, and bilaterality), the adult is more likely to be inclined to step in, too soon, to try to influence behavior.

In such an emotionally toned area as the child's response to his mother or his total response to life situations in general, where the two factors that alternate and interweave are a basic disequilibrium and a basic equilibrium, it is more difficult for the adult to remain objective. Knowledge of approximately when to expect recurring stages of disequilibrium and an appreciation of the fact that a total disequilibrium of response may be expected to characterize certain age levels (regardless of the excellence of environmental conditions or parental handling) can be useful to the parent in guiding the child, and to the pediatrician in guiding the parent.

Though our behavior test norms do not specifically demonstrate this important principle of interweaving, it is useful for parents, teachers, and others who deal with the child in everyday life to be aware that behavior does not necessarily "improve" with age. Figure 1 in Chapter 3, which describes general behavior changes in the years from 1 to 5, demonstrates graphically the way in which ages of equilibrium tend to alternate with ages of disequilibrium during this particular time span.

## DEVELOPMENTAL QUOTIENT VS. INTELLIGENCE QUOTIENT

As will be mentioned later on, it is important for readers to understand that the tests described here yield what we call a Developmental Quotient (DQ) rather than an Intelligence Quotient (IQ); that is, the child's response to our test battery tells us how mature or immature his or her behavior is. The battery indicates whether his responses are congruent with his actual chronological age or are ahead of or behind chronological age, but it does not provide his IQ as such.

In infancy there does appear to be a relatively clear relationship between DQ and IQ. A 9-month-old baby who is responding at a 9-month level of behavior is in all likelihood normally intelligent. Early tests strongly stress the child's motor behavior and, it does appear that in general, although the aim of these tests is not to determine intelligence, they do provide a reasonably good clue as to this attribute.

However, as the child grows older, the two measures of intelligence and maturity may proceed hand in hand or they may diverge sharply. Thus a child might have low intelligence but nevertheless perform at or near his developmental age. Or he may, on so-called tests of intelligence, score well above average, but might on a behavior test show himself to be immature. This leads to the classification we ourselves so often use—"superior-immature"—which means that the child in question is of good or superior intelligence but is still in general ways "young for his age."

As we elaborate in Chapter 13, this distinction is an especially important one when it comes to matters of school placement. Our contention is that, regardless of either birthday age or Intelligence

Quotient, in most instances a child does best in school if started and subsequently promoted on the basis of developmental age. Thus if a 5-year-old child is still behaving like a 4- or 4½-year-old, he will in all likelihood not be ready for the work of kindergarten, regardless of what the law allows.

## FOUR FIELDS OF BEHAVIOR AND DEVELOPMENTAL QUOTIENT

Following our customary methodology, we will present our behavior tests under four separate headings: motor, adaptive, language, and personal-social. These headings speak for themselves. Later in the book a chapter is devoted to each of these kinds of tests.

In figuring the Developmental Quotient, one proceeds as if figuring an Intelligence Quotient. Thus if a 36-month-old child rates at 36 months in motor, adaptive, language, and personal-social behaviors, one divides 36 by 36 and adds two zeros, coming out with a Developmental Quotient of 100.

Let's say there is unevenness—that the 36-month-old child's motor and adaptive behaviors both rate at 42 months, but language and personal-social are, conversely, below his age, rating at 30 months each. One adds the four figures: 42 for motor, 42 for adaptive, 30 for language, and 30 for personal-social. The resulting total is then divided by four (since there are four fields of behavior) and the result again is 36. If this figure is then divided by 36 (the child's age in months), we come out as before with a DQ of 100.

But, and here is the important consideration, the two resulting figures, DQs of 100 each, represent quite different personalities. Examiners will of course definitely be interested in the total DQ, but they may be even more interested in the child's relative strengths in the different fields. The first child mentioned might be expected to be one of rather even temperament, more or less equally endowed in each of the usual fields of behavior. The behavior of the second child tells quite a different story. He or she might be expected to perform, in real-life situations, well above age in motor and adaptive behaviors but below age in both language and personal-social.

Even here, the range is not wide. This hypothetical child is merely a little above age in some areas, below in others. Often we find an even greater range. A third hypothetical child of 36 months might be as low as 24 months in motor, at age in adaptive, as high as 48 months in language and in personal-social. Such a child would end up with a total DQ of 108, but one's expectations of such a child would be rather special. We would realize that his or her very high language and personal-social behaviors, fine in themselves, would provide no real clue as to how this child might perform. His or her low motor and average adaptive behaviors must always be taken into account and allowed for.

In our clinical experience, we find that the wider the range in endowment in the four basic fields of behavior, the harder time the child may have in adapting to living, especially to academic demands. A school situation which fits his high points would be much too demanding for his low points. Conversely, if one suits the school's demands to his lowest points (in this case motor and adaptive behaviors), he will not be well suited when language and personal-social situations are involved. School planning for such a child will have to be highly individual and special.

## INDIVIDUAL DIFFERENCES

This, then, is one aspect of individuality which the examiner will do well to keep in mind—that many children are not evenly endowed in the four major fields of behavior: motor, adaptive, language, and personal-social. Tremendous individual differences may exist as to any child's relative ability in these four fields.

A second area of individual difference which it is essential for any examiner, parent, or teacher to keep in mind is that any norms, such as those provided in this handbook, are only averages. As we have explained in virtually every one of our publications, the reader is urged to remember that *age norms are not set up as standards; they are designed only for orientation and interpretive purposes.* It is a gross misinterpretation of our normative work for anyone to assume that we are saying that all children do or should develop in exactly the same way or at the same rate.

Norms are merely guides to the way that behavior develops in general. They are a statistical device that gives us an average which we can use to measure development. *They are averages but they are not expectations.* Perfectly normal infants and children can vary from our standards by weeks or, as they grow older, even by months, and still not be considered abnormal or atypical.

## THE BASIC USEFULNESS OF TESTING AND OF DIAGNOSIS

For many years psychologists and other behavior specialists, we among them, have busily developed their tests. The value of tests as such was not as a rule disputed. It was merely a question of which tests performed most effectively the tasks for which they were intended, evaluating some aspect of the child's behavior or personality.

Unfortunately, just as tests were being refined to the point where they were, in the minds of many, becoming extremely effective and useful, politics came into the picture. In the interest of protecting everybody's so-called "right to privacy," many, especially those concerned with the rights of underprivileged and/or minority children, began to claim that any psychological testing was an infringement of privacy.

Thus many presumably good-hearted individuals, lacking an understanding of the purpose and usefulness of psychological and behavior testing, came out strongly against testing. Came out so strongly, in fact, that in some big city schools much or most psychological testing has actually been forbidden.

If one were to assume, as some did in the past, that one could make anything of anybody if only one did the "right" thing, then admittedly testing might not be needed. It would not matter what the individual was; it would merely be a matter of helping him or her to become whatever one might wish.

However, if one assumes as we do that behavior is to a large extent determined by inherited biological factors, then the more we know about what the individual is and is not, the better we can help him to come to the fullest expression of his capabilities, and the more effectively we as parents or educators can adapt to his weaknesses. The environment can be fully effective only if it understands what it is working with.

It might help opponents of psychological testing if they could appreciate that a psychological test invades the psyche no more than a physician's physical examination invades the body. The doctor is not expected to fly blind. Nor should the parent, teacher, or psychologist be expected to forgo diagnostic testing.

## MIND MANIFESTS ITSELF

Among our readers there may be those who wonder why, in a book which describes behavior changes in the first six years of life, we say nothing about that popular term—*cognition*. In fact, some may note that we do not speak at any length about the child's *mind*.

The reason for this apparent lack of attention to an aspect of the child's body or behavior that is clearly so important is that we have never thought of the child's mind as something separate from or apart from the rest of him.

"Mind manifests itself" was one of Dr. Arnold Gesell's favorite phrases. As he put it, the child's mind manifests itself in virtually every aspect of his behavior. An infant, who, spying a small sugar pellet, pokes at it with forefinger or grasps it between thumb and forefinger, is giving us an example of his mind at work. He has spied the pellet with his eyes. The wish to obtain that pellet (and probably to put it into his mouth) has made itself felt. His hand carries out the directive of his brain.

That is, it is not by words alone that an infant or preschooler gives evidence of his mind at work. Those of our tests classed under "Language" probably come closest to what many people consider intellectual or mental tests. But to us virtually all of our tests are tests of the child's mind at work. This may be the reason that *cognition* has never become an active part of our vocabulary.

## VIEWING THE WHOLE LIFE SPAN

Since the present volume covers chiefly the first six years of life, a fully detailed description of behavior as it changes year by year is given only for the first six years. However, we should like to give a brief preview of the major changes which take place in the years that follow.

As described elsewhere, it has been our observation that not only do ages of equilibrium alternate with ages of disequilibrium, outgoing ages with inward ages, but that actually in the years from 2 to 5 one can observe a definite and rather elaborate pattern of behavior change.

Interestingly enough, this identical pattern recurs again from 5 to 10 and once more from 10 to 16. The table which follows illustrates the point. It suggests that in the ages between 2 and 16, each of three similar cycles starts with an age of equilibrium. This equilibrium is, thus, seen at 2, 5, and 10 years of age. In each cycle this initial phase of equilibrium is followed by a phase of disequilibrium in which behavior breaks down and becomes oppositional and uncomfortable. These phases of disequilibrium, customarily seen at 2½, 5½, and 11 are followed once again by easy stages, at 3, 6½, and 12 years, during which things tend to go well.

Once again, at a succeeding stage, behavior breaks down and is characterized by insecurity and withdrawal. The 3½-year-old tends to be extremely insecure in every way. The 7-year-old often seems unhappy, thinks that people do not like him. Thirteen withdraws and goes his own way.

Withdrawal is followed by expansion and, in general, behavior tends to be extremely expansive at 4, 8, and 14 years of age. Once again we come to stages of insecurity, disequilibrium, unpredictableness at 4½, 9, and 15 and then finally end up with equilibrium at 5, 10, and 16 years of age.

TABLE 1

STAGES OF EQUILIBRIUM AND DISEQUILIBRIUM

| EVEN | BREAKUP | CALM | WITHDRAWAL | EXPANSION | TRANSITION | EQUILIBRIUM |
|---|---|---|---|---|---|---|
| 2 | 2½ | 3 | 3½ | 4 | 4½ | 5 |
| 5 | 5½–6 | 6½ | 7 | 8 | 9 | 10 |
| 10 | 11 | 12 | 13 | 14 | 15 | 16 |

It has been our impression that predictable and patterned behavior changes continue throughout the entire life span. This has been our contention, though our own work has not documented any such fact. This lack is due perhaps to the fact that we have not studied in any detail the middle years of life. Rather, we have confined our research chiefly to the first 16 years and the years from 70 to the end of life.

Our research on old age (17) has suggested that behavior of the elderly person tends to change with age in almost the exact reverse of the way it builds up in the young. We then picture the changes in behavior which can be observed over the entire life span as an elongated diamond.

In the earliest years, the first 16 to 20, basic behaviors such as can be measured by our kinds of tests open up, expand, become increasingly mature and effective. Then, for most, or many, they remain fairly stable until the individual is somewhere around 65 or 70. After that, for many, behavior begins to deteriorate and to become less active or effective.

In the early years of life, in spite of marked and important individual differences, chronological age provides a reasonably good clue as to what one may expect. We find it meaningful to speak of 3-year-old behavior, 4-year-old behavior, and the like. Toward the end of life, individual differences are so much greater that chronological age provides a less effective clue as to what kind of behavior to expect. Thus instead of talking about 70-year-old behavior or 80-year-old behavior, we instead speak of behavior in terms of stages, as follows:

*Intact Adult:* This behavior, regardless of the subject's age, resembles that of the mature adult, with few or no signs of deterioration.

*Intact Presenile*: Such an individual remains reasonably effective—may, for instance, manage and maintain his or her own home—but small signs of the breakup of behavior do appear.

*Medium Presenile*: This stage covers a rather wide range of behavior possibilities. At its most intact end, the individual may present a plausible social appearance, but judgment may become questionable, perceptions not very clear. At its most feeble end, the individual, though still in touch with the world around him, needs considerable protection and supervision.

*Senile*: Such individuals are in very poor touch with reality. Their behavior rates on our tests in the 3- to 5-year-old range.

The signs of deterioration which accompany and identify these changes can be measured objectively by means of our own preschool and school-age tests: Cubes, Copy Forms, Incomplete Man, Visual Three, and also by the Bender-Gestalt. Other tests useful in determining levels of deterioration or intactness are the Rorschach, the Mosaic, and the Color Tree Test.

A graphic presentation of the entire life span, as we see it, resembles an elongated diamond:

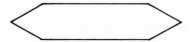

Until just recently, behavior changes which might be exhibited during the middle years remained a mystery. Now, thanks to the careful scientific work of Daniel Levinson of Yale (53), as well as the popularization of that work by Gail Sheehy (60), even this mystery is being cleared up.

Dr. Gesell, in a 1956 interview with *Time* magazine, commented that "Our present-day knowledge of the (child's) mind is like a 15th-century map of the world, a mixture of truth and error. There are scattered islands of dependable fact, but there are still unknown continents." Now that map is becoming clearer and more precise.

The chapters which immediately follow present for parents and others interested primarily in the home behavior of the whole child a detailed description month by month in the first year of life, half year by half year in the years from 1 to 6.

In Part Two we describe individually the tests which make up our own scale of motor, adaptive, language, and personal-social behavior.

In Part Three we present our norms, as well as samples of the behavior schedules which an examiner can use in rating a child's behavioral response. We also give suggestions to smooth an examiner's way in giving a developmental examination. A chapter on so-called "Variant Behavior" helps an examiner to appreciate that even when a child is not responding positively to an examination, his manner of refusing provides good clues as to his or her developmental level.

And finally in Part Four we emphasize sex and group differences which we have observed and discuss various uses to which the Gesell Behavior Examination can be put.

# 2

## The First Year of Life

The title of this book promises information on the first year of life, as well as the years that follow. However, tests and examination techniques described here begin at 2½ years of age. Our emphasis is thus admittedly more on the second half of the preschool period than on the first.

Examiners interested in the developmental examination of infants and children younger than 2½ years of age are referred to an earlier book by Gesell and Amatruda, currently edited by Knobloch and Pasamanick, entitled *Developmental Diagnosis* (33). Parents and others especially interested in the details of behavior in the first year of life may wish to consult our revised edition of *Infant and Child in the Culture of Today* (35).

A brief survey of motor behavior, adaptive behavior, language behavior, and self-activity in the first year of life is given here in tabular form with emphasis on the ages 4 weeks, 16 weeks, 28 weeks, 40 weeks, and 52 weeks. (See Table 2.)

## TABLE 2

### DEVELOPMENT DURING THE FIRST YEAR

| | WHOLE BODY ACTIVITY | ADAPTIVE BEHAVIOR: USE OF FINGERS AND HANDS | LANGUAGE AND SOCIAL ACTIVITY | SELF-ACTIVITY |
|---|---|---|---|---|
| 4 WEEKS | Cannot sit, stand, creep, or walk. When on stomach, can lift head slightly. If propped or held in sitting position, head sags. When on back, may turn head to one side. In fact, may prefer head on side. From about 4–16 weeks, fencing position appears—head turned to one side with arm on that side extended and the other arm bent upward. May roll or wriggle part way to one side. Most prefer to lie on their back. | Responds mostly with eyes. Lying on back, looks at things overhead. Objects or fingers placed inside baby's own are grasped—this is a reflex action, not voluntary. | Has few social responses at this early age. Smiles may be only gas pain smiles. May make small, throaty sounds. May pay attention to voices and seem to enjoy being bathed. | Mostly just lies on back, looking at things, and turning head a little from side to side. Crying may be the most active movement, except for eating and sleeping. |

|  | Whole Body Activity | Adaptive Behavior: Use of Fingers and Hands | Language and Social Activity | Self-Activity |
|---|---|---|---|---|
| **16 Weeks** | Fencing position begins to disappear. Both arms are most often in the same position, and head is more in midline. When on back, can hold head steady. When on stomach, though still cannot progress, can take a swimming position with weight on abdomen only, legs extended and lifted, head and arms lifted high. Can sit propped, head no longer dropping forward. Many now seem to enjoy lying on their back as well as on their stomach. | Adaptive behavior still limited. Will look at things overhead if lying on back. Or if sitting, will regard objects placed before him, often looking from hand to object to hand. Arms move as infant sees an object, but still cannot grasp it. Arm movement is of the whole hand. Back of hand may thus touch object. | Baby now smiles and laughs, coos, chuckles, and gurgles. Notices voices and recognizes care-givers, especially mother. Likes to sit up (propped) and loves attention. | May still lie mostly on back but can kick forcefully, turning head actively from side to side. Can roll to one side. May manage to touch or grasp objects hung overhead if they are placed in hand. Loves to play with own hands. Eyes may still be more active than hands—that is, "grasps" with eyes. |
| **28 Weeks** | Most can lift legs high while lying on back. May even grasp feet. Also can roll onto stomach. Most now prefer to lie on stomach. Still cannot creep or crawl but on verge of turning in circles. Most can sit erect momentarily. Can take a large part of own weight if held erect and can bounce up and down actively. This is an "almost" stage: can almost turn in circles, almost sit, almost take own weight. | Hands now become tools with which to explore objects. Can reach for object and grasp it in a crude grasp. Can bang object on table top; can transfer it from hand to hand. May grasp two objects at one time—one in each hand. Still cannot pick up tiny objects, such as crumbs. | Now can distinguish between people he knows and strangers. Laughs, gurgles, coos with familiar people. May even say *mmm*. Likes to sit propped, to be held, carried, bounced on somebody's knee, or taken for a carriage ride. May even pat own image in mirror. | Still may lie on back though prefers prone. While on stomach, thrusts one knee forward. May like to roll over. Plays with feet. Loves to handle a bell, rattle, ball, or rubber squeaky toy. Likes to bite. Brings most everything to his mouth. Loves to vocalize. |

| | Whole Body Activity | Adaptive Behavior: Use of Fingers and Hands | Language and Social Activity | Self-Activity |
|---|---|---|---|---|
| 40 Weeks | Most no longer lie on their back except perhaps to sleep. Now in prone position, can turn in circles, crawl by pulling weight over forearms. Can get to hands and knees (soon will creep). Can sit steady for long periods and can go from sitting to prone. Can pull to feet by side of playpen. | Hands now much more skillful than earlier. Instead of earlier pawlike grasp, can now grasp more skillfully and can poke with forefinger. Can bang two blocks together. Can wave or shake a rattle, no longer just by chance. | Now very social. Responds to nursery games. Can play pat-a-cake and perhaps wave bye-bye. Loves to play and be played with. Loves to "talk." Vocabulary may include *Mama, Dada,* and perhaps one other "word." | Major kind of self-activity is still motor. Very active motorwise. Can sit up, lean over, and sit up again. Can pull to standing. Can crawl and almost creep. Likes to vocalize and is very responsive socially. An age of experiment. Loves to handle objects. |
| 52 Weeks | Creeping, now perfected, is a favorite activity. "Into" everything. Most can now stand alone; can cruise by side of playpen. May walk with one hand held. | Big advance in manipulative skills. Can even try to pile one block on another. Can put a small pellet into a bottle. Can pick up small objects, such as crumbs. | Now is truly sociable. Enjoys being hugged, talked to, laughed with. Loves pat-a-cake, bye-bye, "Where's the baby?" Enjoys rhymes. Loves to creep and chase things. Throws things from high chair. Will give a toy if asked. May even cooperate in dressing. | Self-activity now extremely varied. Likes to look, touch, grasp, handle, manipulate, combine objects. Loves to move about in space. Likes to vocalize, to socialize. Very responsive to other people. |

# 3

# From One to Six Years

In the many years that we have worked with children, we have come to an increasing realization that the behavior which a child expresses at any given age amounts to a great deal more than the sum of the separate things he can do.

We have determined, at least to our own satisfaction, that each

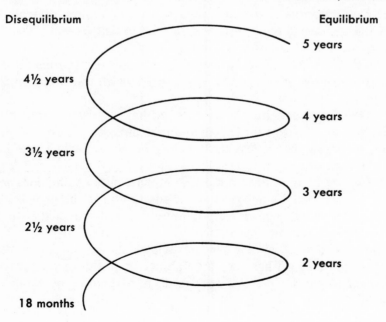

**Disequilibrium**                                    **Equilibrium**

                                                        5 years

4½ years

                                                        4 years

3½ years

                                                        3 years

2½ years

                                                        2 years

18 months

FIGURE I *Alternation of Ages of Equilibirium and Disequilibrium*

age, like each boy or girl, has an individuality of its own.* Some ages are calm, others explosive. At some ages the child seems to be in good equilibrium; at others, in rather marked disequilibrium. There are ages when he is compliant and restrained; others when behavior is definitely out of bounds.

All of this occurs in such a systematic way and so similarly from child to child that we have come to think of developing behavior as spiraling upward, now at one of two extremes, now at the other. Figure 1 indicates our view of these alternations as they occur in the first six years of life.

This of course does not mean that all 2½-year-olds are difficult at all times or in all situations, or that all THREES are continually calm and amenable. Behavior can vary from hour to hour as it does from child to child. But in general we have found these characterizations to hold and to help in our understanding of the inevitable behavior changes which will take place as any given child matures.


## THE 18-MONTHER

Eighteen months is a time which can be extremely difficult for even the gentlest boy or girl, and for the parent as well. The 18-monther wants what he wants and he wants it *now*.

It is hard for him to accept any delay or failure. And his failures tend to be many because of his immaturity in almost every field of behavior.

His wants are definite but he does not have the words to express them, and thus, except for crying and tantrums, he has no good way to let you know that it was the blue bib he wanted when you gave him the pink one.

Motorwise he may have almost as much trouble as he does with language. His body is not yet quite ready to do the things he wants of it. Emotionally, too, his very definite demands coupled with his lack of "give" get him into difficulty.

And most important of all his personal-social relations give difficulty, since he as yet has very little ability to do things your way or to do something he does not want to do just because you want him to do it.

*See also Arnold Gesell, Frances L. Ilg, and Louise B. Ames, *Infant and Child in the Culture of Today*, rev. ed. (New York: Harper & Row, 1974). Also, Louise B. Ames and Frances L. Ilg, *Your Two Year Old, Your Three Year Old, Your Four Year Old, Your Five Year Old*, and *Your Six Year Old* (New York: Delacorte, 1976 and 1979).

Life can be very hard for the child of this age. Certainly he has changed a great deal since he was a mere 1 year of age. Physically, especially, he is very different. He has gained from two to three inches in height and as many pounds in weight; he may have twice as many teeth as he did just six months before. He may still sleep as much as 13 hours, or over half the time, but usually has given up one of his two daily naps.

## MOTOR BEHAVIOR

Now the child walks well; he even runs, though admittedly with some stiffness. One of the interesting things about the body at this age is that it does not always bend. Try stuffing an 18-monther into his high chair and he stiffens like a ramrod. Try to cuddle him in your lap and he straightens out and slides off. But he can walk up stairs, with help or if there is a railing, and he can also descend stairs without difficulty.

He not only can get himself around but he can push his favorite push-toy, pull his favorite pull-toy as he walks.

He can seat himself on a small chair, though perhaps by backing into it. If asked to kick a ball, he can at least walk into it, even though he cannot as yet really kick.

## ADAPTIVE BEHAVIOR

Hands are now used rather effectively. Even though they are not as yet really skillful, most 18-monthers can manage a tower of three and can pile round, triangular, and square blocks on a formboard even though not as yet place them in their proper holes.

EIGHTEEN can usually turn a few pages of a (large) picture book. Given a crayon and paper, he will scribble spontaneously and may even imitate a stroke.

## LANGUAGE BEHAVIOR

Language varies tremendously from one child to another, but it is not unusual for an 18-monther to have as many as ten words (or maybe more), including "Mama," "Dada," and proper names. He can usually, in a test situation, follow two directions with a ball, giving it to Mother (or throwing it at her) and putting it on (or throwing it at) a table or chair.

Many, when shown a picture book, can name or point to the doggie, kitty, baby, or other familiar object or person. When out for a walk, they enjoy having someone else point out interesting aspects of the environment.

Some highly verbal boys and girls at this age, instead of talking in intelligible words, jargon fluently. Perhaps more characteristic is the one-word sentence: "Coat," "Hat," "Out." Eighteen also responds best if addressed in very simple, sparse language.

His own best word is definitely "No." Comprehension may exceed verbalization. Many seem to understand a great deal of what is said to them. Many now quite easily (if in the mood) obey simple commands such as "Come," "Out," "Walk," "Give it to me." And most can understand, though they do not always obey "No, no."

### PERSONAL-SOCIAL BEHAVIOR

The 1-year-old child has not yet reached a concept of personal belonging. He may easily give up his toy to a demanding older friend or sibling. The 18-monther is beginning to claim *mine* and to be grabby. Ordinarily very content in self-absorbed spontaneous play, he shows enthusiastic and persistent interest in almost anything that comes his way. Even a little crumb on the floor may hold his attention for quite some time; in fact, almost any object or person that comes his way may attract his interest, even though he often treats other children more as objects than as people.

He tends to be extremely resistant to change and to any and all sudden transitions. He avoids them by physically refusing to cooperate, even by running away or by just plain tantrums. And though not necessarily possessive of toys, he may strenuously object if even Mother or Grandmother puts her hand on the arm of his chair.

This is a very awkward, negativistic age. Demands are strong. Ability to convey them is weak. Ability to adapt to the requirements of others is almost nonexistent.

So here we have a little organism who wants what he wants and wants it *now*. But one who cannot tell you exactly what it is that he wants, cannot brook delay, most certainly cannot comply. The result, all too often, is impasse!

And yet many capable, even endearing characteristics now make themselves apparent. The child will often at mealtimes hand you his empty dish, with a smile, instead of, when finished, throwing it onto the floor as earlier.

He "loves" his dolly or teddy bear and may share them or may not. Many at least "help" feed themselves. Some are already dry after their nap even though by no means all day long.

It has been remarked that the typical 18-monther often performs like an automaton, and some parents feel that it is, at least part of the time, possible to "program" him.

Eighteen also at times seems to think with his feet. Instead of seeing an object and making for it, he often notices it after he has bumped into it in his seemingly aimless bumbling about the room.

The secret of success, for the adult, may be not to approach this interesting little creature head-on. If you want him to come where you are, do *not* say "Come here, dear." Rather, lure him by holding out a cookie or favorite toy, or turn your back and crumple some paper or make other interesting noises. (Then he may toddle over to see what you are doing.) Or perhaps simplest of all, merely approach him from behind and without talking about it, lift him over to where you want him to be.

What is required for successful or even mildly comfortable living is not only a sixth sense—a sort of intuitive understanding of what the child actually requires—but also a great willingness to give, to adapt, to let live, on the parents' part.

This is, admittedly, one of the first really difficult ages. The child seems to be all "want" and no "give." "Bad boy" and "No" may be his favorite expressions. Soon, fortunately, things will improve on almost every front: motorwise the child will become more secure; languagewise he will have the words, or at least some of the words, that he needs to tell you what he wants.

Emotionally he will soon, if one is fortunate, move over to the positive side of life. Adaptively, too, things will improve. Objects will do what he wants them to do as hands and eyes become increasingly skilled and cooperate better with his intent.

## THE 2- AND THE 2½-YEAR-OLD

"The Terrible Twos" is a phrase used all too often, and all too often incorrectly. It has come about through a misinterpretation of what we ourselves have had to say.

In our experience the average 2-year-old is a creature of considerable good will, often quite willing and able to conform to the demands of those around him.

This increased conformity, compared to where he was some six months earlier, has come about chiefly because life is so much easier for him than it used to be. Now he has rather good control of his body, is much more able to do what he wants to do; that is, to an increasing extent, he can count on it. He falls much less often, walks easily, even runs. He talks more easily. Much of the time he is able to name the things he wants. Emotionally he is on a more even keel. And socially too things are going better. Most of the time he and those around him are very much in tune.

If all of this is true, why then the term "Terrible Twos"? It came about, in all likelihood because, following the growth pattern depicted in Figure 1, the trends of growth at 2½ move the child from the calm and equilibrium so delightfully characteristic of 2 to a temporary stage of discomfort and disequilibrium which seems to characterize the age of 2½.

For a brief time then many a growing boy or girl is indeed "terrible." Life is hard for him and for those around him. As will be described below in more detail, the typical 2½-year-old lives a life of opposite extremes. Whatever one wants him to do—or even what he himself wants to do—will be followed shortly, if not immediately, by his wish to do exactly the opposite.

He is also characteristically rigid and ritualistic, bossy and demanding, altogether determined to have his own way. And he tends to resent any change. He is not an easy person to be or to be with.

Thus we shall, under this general age heading, describe two quite different individuals—the typically gentle and easy-to-get-on-with 2-year-old and his own just older self, the difficult, demanding 2½-year-old.

## MOTOR BEHAVIOR

The typical TWO has improved greatly in the past six months, so far as motor skills are concerned. He walks well and even runs. He needs no help in climbing up and down stairs and can even jump from the lowest step. Though his gait is no longer a baby stagger or toddle, it is still short-stepped and constrained compared to what it will be later on.

At 18 months many a child would ride in his carriage for as long as somebody was willing to push him. Now at 2 years, he may wish to get out and push his own carriage.

He can kick a ball, not just walk into it. He can walk very steadily. He can push a toy with good steering. However, motor behavior, whether of arms or legs or total body or merely of fingers, is still broadly undifferentiated. Thus TWO's gait is constrained because of lack of freedom at both ankle and knee, so that he tends to walk with an up-and-down tread. Foot and leg move as one rather than as articulated parts whose different motions will later be integrated into a smooth walking pattern.

Motor behavior, though now much enjoyed, is apt to be undertaken for its own sake rather than because of the goal involved. Thus TWO may climb stairs or climb on a jungle gym as much for the pleasure of climbing as because he wants to get to the top.

Manual control has improved to the point where he can turn the pages of a book rather skillfully, can build a tower of six or seven small blocks, can imitate the drawing of a vertical stroke. But he still has trouble in using one hand independently of the other. If he holds out an injured finger for bandaging, he is likely to hold out his other hand as well.

But he can use fingers skillfully enough to be able to put together large, simple puzzles, or paint and crayon (even though with whole-arm movements). He (or she) can string large beads, unscrew the lids of jars, manipulate Play Doh.

The 18-monther holds a glass of milk with two hands and often precariously. TWO may hold it quite effectively in one hand only, though his other hand remains poised to help out in case of need.

By 2½, motor abilities have come an even longer way. Coordination has increased to the point where the child can walk on tiptoes, can jump with both feet, can even attempt, when so requested, to stand on one foot. Many can now throw a ball, catch a ball (with arms and body combined), kick a ball with ease.

Fine motor behavior, too, has improved to the extent that the child can now build a tower of ten, imitate a horizontal and circular as well as a vertical stroke.

Significantly, fingers are now increasingly differentiated from the hand as a whole and are less likely to open or close as a unit. This is especially helpful when one is trying to put on his mittens.

In manipulating objects, improvement is not startling—mostly, each of the earlier fine motor abilities is increasing and smoothing out. He (or she) strings beads more skillfully. Or painting shows increasing effectiveness of wrist motion, less of the whole-arm movement seen at 2 years.

For many, handedness is not yet clearly decided. The child may shift an object from hand to hand, or the hand he uses may be determined by which side the spoon or other object is placed on. It is not till 3 years or later that many establish handedness.

## ADAPTIVE BEHAVIOR

TWO builds a tower of twice as many blocks as he could manage six months earlier. Now he can manage a tower of six or seven, and line up three blocks to make a train. By 2½ he can build a tower of ten and can add a chimney or smokestack to his train. In fact, in infancy and early childhood it seems to take about six months of neurological growth before a child can do something distinctly new in his exploitation of cubes, as shown by the following table:

### TABLE 3

### AGE CHANGES IN RESPONSE TO CUBES

1 month : Grasps a cube on contact, but does not seem to see it.
6 months: Grasps a cube directly on seeing it.
12 months: Brings one cube over another, without release.
18 months: Places three cubes one on the other to make a tower of three.
24 months: Places three cubes in a row to make a "train."
30 months: Places a chimney cube on his train.
36 months: Builds a bridge of three cubes.
48 months: Imitates a "gate" of five cubes.
60 months: Builds a two-step staircase.
72 months: Builds a three-step staircase.

TWO loves to touch, to taste, to smell, to feel. All his senses seem used even more than in the months just earlier. He is a real explorer. That may be why it takes him so long, when out for a walk, to cover even a short distance. He has to come into contact with everything that presents itself along the way.

TWO loves the things he does indoors, too. He loves to paint and model with clay, even though his products are extremely rudimentary. He loves to fill his pail or dish with sand or stones, dumping and throwing. And if permitted, he adores water play.

He enjoys looking at books, especially simple books with big, clear, uncluttered pictures. He especially enjoys his own books, particularly small books, and actually may get as much fun out of carrying them around with him as in looking at them.

Doll play is a favorite of both boys and girls, though at this age it is not very complicated. Just putting the doll to bed and covering it with a piece of cloth may be about as far as he (or she) wishes to go. Or, even without dolls, boys and girls enjoy any simple domestic play which imitates the events in their own daily life, such as eating and sleeping.

TWO can appropriately place a single block on a formboard which has three holes of circular, square, and triangular forms. TWO-AND-A-HALF can fit all three blocks into their proper holes if the blocks are presented under their matching holes. And if the formboard is then rotated so that the blocks are not under their matching holes, he can adapt to this rotation, even though with occasional error.

Response to puzzles becomes increasingly effective. He can now manage puzzles with several rather complicated parts. Play Doh products, though still very simple, take on increasing shape and structure.

By 2½ years of age, adaptive behavior has improved by leaps and bounds—not so much in type as in quality—over what it was at 2. It is in his increasing mastery of simple materials that the older child shows his superiority over what he was just earlier.

As one can easily observe, manipulative behavior becomes increasingly skillful. Bead stringing is now more effective, and fewer beads are dropped. Painting involves more purposeful wrist motion and less whole-arm stroking.

Adaptive behavior involving fine motor coordination and play in general are much less bumbling than six months earlier. Now boy or girl shows considerable skill in putting together stacking toys of all kinds. Things work better for him than they did just earlier. He can sometimes even figure out how to solve small problems that arise in the course of his play.

## LANGUAGE BEHAVIOR

There is perhaps no more exciting time in the growth of language behavior than the period between 2 and 2½ years of age.

The 18-monther usually has a few handy words at his command, but all of a sudden, at 2, words come tumbling out of his mouth.

Just earlier, if quite communicative, he may have managed what we call one-word sentences—the single word that effectively takes the place of a sentence: Eat, Sit, Read, Ride. "No" remains strong as does that most useful of all words, "Mine." Now at 2 those individual words have multiplied, in the verbal child, to several hundred. He has names for almost everything and he takes pleasure and pride in naming people, animals, or things pointed out to him in his picture books.

Most at 2 years are well beyond the jargon stage, and many now speak in simple three-word sentences. Though parts of speech mean little yet, the 2-year-old often uses not only nouns but also prepositions and verbs. He may use pronouns correctly though "Me" is still favored over "I" in reference to self. (Or the child may refer to himself by his proper name, as earlier.)

Some may still confuse animate and inanimate and may jabber away at inanimate objects. And even when alone the child may try out verbal sound effects just for the fun of it.

Typical of the language of 2-year-olds are such phrases as "Here's a car car," "Too many people," "Me climb," "Watch me," "Where Mommy?" "Where baw?" Or the child may report on his own activities as "Me show Mommy leaf."

The typical 2-year-old loves to be read to. He prefers books which tell about the kinds of simple, daily activities that he himself engages in. He especially likes books with repetitive phrases such as "Good night clock," "Good night chair," "Good night door," "Good night Mommy."

Language is not only useful at 2; it is also fun. But much more, language is directed toward adults rather than other children.

However, as versatile as language can be at 2, it is somewhat one-way since the child most enjoys language that is initiated by self. What a change at 2½! Now language is only part of the time self-initiated; often it is also responsive.

The child can now tell you his or her name and also (if a girl) her sex. (Boys tend to be six months later in the ability to identify own sex.) He or she can also obey such requests as putting a ball *on* or *under* a chair, and is increasingly good at naming pictured objects.

The use of "me" has in most quite fully taken the place of the child's proper name, and highly verbal children may even refer to themselves as "I."

Now the child talks to (though not necessarily with) other children as well as, though not as much as, to adults. He is coming to realize, even more than he did six months earlier, what a useful and enjoyable tool language can be.

Vocabulary has increased by leaps and bounds. Long gone is jargon. Long past, the use of the one-word sentence. The child can now, in short sentences, announce current, completed, or intended activity *: "Me fix it," "Me make it go," "I want to climb." Or he will ask for help: "I need to get down. Help me." He loves to brag about his own prowess: "I can take my coat off."

He gives information freely: "I have beads at my house." He loves to command the adult: "Hey, get out of my way" or "Get some for me." He also bosses other children: "Ann, get off. Use this one," "Get outta here, Bill." Or, more politely: "Me need one of these. Sank you" or even "Let me help you."

That highly verbal activity, being read to, is becoming ever more of a pleasure, for child if not for adult. The 2½-year-old dearly loves to be read to, but now reading may be a little trying for the grownup since the child will not allow the skipping of a single word or sentence, no matter how tedious the story. And for many, once is not enough. As one 2½-year-old put it, "And when you're finished, you'll read it again and again and again."

All in all, in most children, especially girls, language has become not only a highly effective means of communication but a pleasure as well.

## PERSONAL-SOCIAL BEHAVIOR

Possibly the most conspicuous differences between 2 and 2½ years are those that can be seen in the area of personal-social behavior. TWO is still just out of babyhood. TWO-AND-A-HALF is very much a person in his own right.

TWO tends to be gentle, docile, and conforming. TWO-AND-A-HALF is rigid, ritualistic, demanding, oppositional, and altogether difficult, even though he can do many things that he could not do six months earlier. TWO cooperates. TWO-AND-A-HALF can be at a high point of negativism. TWO is beginning to help in dressing himself—at least he can pull on a simple garmet. The 2½-year-old can go much further. He can locate armholes, pull off leggings and socks, and is beginning to take an interest in buttons and buttonholes.

TWO uses a spoon without excessive spilling. TWO-AND-A-HALF

*Adapted from Louise B. Ames and Frances L. Ilg, *Your Two Year Old* (New York: Delacorte Press, 1976).

can go quite a way toward feeding himself. He gives trouble, though, as to what he will eat. Whatever kind of food is offered, he tends to want something different. And if *that* is provided, his preference may shift back to the first thing offered.

Most TWOS have reached no more than the beginning of interest in toileting. Many 2½-year-olds may actually have achieved both bowel and bladder control. TWO may go to bed with relative ease but, once in bed, characteristically makes many demands for a drink, the bathroom, another kiss. Six months later the problem may be not so much one of getting him to stay in bed and to cease demands as getting him *into* bed. This is the age when elaborate bedtime rituals, repeated nightly, may become necessary even though fatiguing to a tired parent.

Socially, TWO may like the company of other children and may enjoy standing side by side with some other, both playing quietly with sand or Play Doh, but there tends to be little interaction. Any grouping may be brief, fluid, and almost impersonal. TWO-AND-A-HALF does interact, but it is apt to be in a somewhat negative way, since the typical 2½-year-old wants to (and seems to need to) hold onto any toy or object that he is playing with, has played with, or might in the future want to play with. Cooperation and sharing have not yet made their appearance.

In fact there tends to be considerable hitting, slapping, pushing, and grabbing. The social life of the child of this age is not particularly harmonious.

However, many at 2½ will accept help from an adult in the form of suggestion: "You can have it when he's through," "What else could you use?" "It's his turn now." Good cooperative social play is in the offing, but for most it is not yet securely here and parallel play remains the order of the day. If successful group play is to take place at this age, it will require considerable adult supervision and intervention.

## THE 3- AND THE 3½-YEAR-OLD

THREE and THREE-AND-A-HALF provide one further example of a pair of ages close in time but far apart in behavior characteristics. Three is for many an age of delightful conformity, happy sharing, comfortable interpersonal relationships. Three-and-a-half, by contrast, tends to be one of those times when the child has trouble not only within himself, but also with almost everybody around him.

The contrast, in many, is very sharp. THREE obeys and is pleased with his obedience. THREE-AND-A-HALF disobeys and grows shrill in his disobedience. Life is easy for THREE; difficult indeed for THREE-AND-A-HALF. THREE seems to feel secure as he (or she) takes life as it is. For THREE-AND-A-HALF, insecurity, yet a need to have one's own way, brings a fight at every step.

The typical 3-year-old goes his way serenely, happy with the world. The typical 3½-year-old, in contrast, tends to be a child who is characteristically inward-turning, insecure, anxious but at the same time determined and self-willed.

As Figure 1 suggests, 3 is a time of good equilibrium; 3½, a time of disequilibrium.

## MOTOR BEHAVIOR

These contrasts are seen very clearly in all four fields of behavior. Motorwise, THREE is in good balance and in good control in both gross and fine motor behaviors. He walks and runs easily and surely, with good balance; he can even walk on tiptoe. He has control of his own speed. He can jump down from a bottom step with both feet together. At 2 he jumped with one foot leading the other. He now easily alternates his feet when going upstairs. And he can even stand on one foot momentarily. He can, and does with great pleasure, ride his tricycle.

Hands are in as good control as are legs and total body. THREE, like his predecessor, can build a sturdy tower of ten blocks, can imitate a three-cube bridge so surely that the top cube stays nicely in place.

In contrast, somewhat surprisingly for those who assume that added age brings added ability, the 3½-year-old is much less secure and effective physically. He often stumbles, frequently falls. Even when he does not actually fall, he shows a fear of falling, as when descending a flight of stairs.

Even his tower of cubes, so secure six months earlier, may fall as his now trembling hand insecurely places cube on cube. He has much more difficulty than just earlier in balancing the center cube of the bridge.

And along with other "going-to-pieces" bits of behavior typical of this age, some boys and girls go so far as to blink their eyes, twitch their faces. This is an age characterized by stuttering, stumbling, trembling, and ticlike behavior in what we assume to be perfectly normal boys and girls.

Thus the older child may be abler, but the characteristic insecurity of THREE-AND-A-HALF causes him to approach almost any task with less assurance than he showed when he was merely THREE.

## ADAPTIVE BEHAVIOR

In this field, too, we see sharp contrasts between the two ages. THREE-AND-A-HALF can do many more things than THREE can, but again his insecurity often makes him seem less able. As mentioned above, his often trembling hand makes any block-building task more precarious. Even his pencil stroke may be light and wavering, in contrast to the 3-year-old's much bolder, surer stroke.

However, as would be expected, when it comes to specific task-oriented achievements, it is THREE-AND-A-HALF who has the advantage. THREE can imitate (but not copy) a bridge of three cubes

, copy a circle, imitate a cross, add three parts to our Incomplete Man form, adapt to the rotation of our formboard (which has three holes—round, triangular, square) with no error or immediate correction of error.

THREE-AND-A-HALF can build the bridge of three cubes from a model (that is, he does not need to see it being built), can copy a cross, add four parts to the Incomplete Man.

That is, his abilities have increased. But his personality problems—his insecurity, yet his strong need to succeed and to have things his own way—sometimes make it difficult for him to put his increased abilities to effective use.

## LANGUAGE BEHAVIOR

In this field as well as in others, we see the interesting paradox of the behavior changes which take place between 3 and 3½ years of age. The 3½-year-old obviously has more words and a greater command of language than does the 3-year-old. Yet it is THREE-AND-A-HALF, not THREE, who, just as he stumbles and trembles, also stutters. Stuttering at this time of life seems to us not so much a specific speech deficiency as a typical example of the insecurity of the 3½-year-old. Even his speech is affected by his insecurity.

But in spite of some stuttering and some hesitancy, the 3½-year-old obviously expresses many verbal abilities not yet acquired by the 3-year-old. Thus he can obey four prepositions in the ball and chair test whereas THREE could manage only three. He can repeat three digits in two out of three trials whereas THREE repeats three digits only once out of three trials.

In the so-called Action Agent test ("What scratches, sleeps, flies, bites, etc.?"), he can respond to 12 questions correctly whereas at 3, he managed only six to seven. That is, he can do more with his language in a typical behavior test situation.

In everyday living there are also clearly observable differences. Jargon at 18 months, words at 2 years, sentences at 2½. And, of course, even longer sentences at 3 and 3½. By then most children can say just about anything they want to or need to.

At 3 years of age, for the first time, the child's conversation is directed as much toward other children as adults; language thus becomes truly reciprocal. Children now talk *with,* not just *to,* other children.

THREE still talks to himself at times, confirming his own activity: "Now I put dis block on dis udder one." He tells grownups what he is doing, asks questions, seeks permission.

And socially with other children he talks about things they will do together: "Let's make b'leeve dis is a store." Or may even project into the future: "Jamie, I wonder. I wish you'd come to my house sometime. I wish you'd bring your bike."

Language at 3½ is not entirely different—only more so. Now there is less use of the infantile "dis" since most can say "this." "Me" as a way of referring to self has definitely been superseded by "I." And we see here the beginnings of correct grammatical usage, including the use of auxiliary verbs such as "would," "could," "be," "have," "can." And the 3½-year-old uses the negative very effectively: "I don't want to."

Even at 3 and increasingly at 3½ the boy or girl shows a love of language for its own sake, and is effectively motivated if addressed with just the right word. Anything described by the adult as "new," "wonderful," "different," "a surprise," or "a secret" will be well accepted and appreciated, even though it may be no more "wonderful" or "different" than a graham cracker.

THREE-AND-A-HALF is especially responsive to voice inflection, especially to whispered instructions which he may follow better than those given in a normal tone of voice.

The child's love of language at both 3 and 3½ makes these ideal times for reading to him. No one could be a more appreciative listener.

Questioning, which will increase at 4, is already beginning in earnest. At 3, and even more so at 3½, the child will want to know Why? How? What? When?

According to Laurie and Joseph Braga (21), in the age period between 3 and 4 years, children begin to use most of the sounds of their language fairly well. Most English-speaking American children use about 90% of the American English vowels during this time. The size of the vocabulary varies from child to child. A guess as to the average size of vocabulary for the 3-year-old might be at least 1,000 words; for the 3½-year-old, 1,200.

Though some children even at 3½ still use "infantile articulation" —they especially say "dis" for "this" and "wide" for "ride"—most can be understood quite easily even by people outside the family.

Social conversation at 3½ is, predictably, even more advanced than it was six months earlier. Now the child may make actual "sharing" talk with friends: "Let me have yours and you have mine. That would be a good thing." Or "You hold one side and I'll hold the other." Language is truly coming into its own.

## PERSONAL- SOCIAL AND EMOTIONAL BEHAVIOR

It is in the realm of emotional and personal-social behavior that the child of this age level shows perhaps the greatest gains over his younger self—and also the greatest contrasts between 3 and 3½.

Take eating behavior, for instance. The typical 3-year-old is rather good at feeding himself and proud of his ability. Filling the spoon is done rather easily by most, even though there may still be a little spilling. And most can hold cup or glass with only one hand instead of two. Food preferences are less marked than earlier and, if the parent is careful not to push, refusals may be relatively few.

How different at 3½ when a typical mother may say, "I dread to get up in the morning and face the thought of getting three meals into my daughter before bedtime!" For many, nothing about the meal is right. They object to the type of food offered, the amount, the way it is put on the plate, and even the way the sandwich is cut. (They want it crosswise instead of up and down.) Mealtime can indeed be a battle.

Dressing, like eating, shows the same contrasts. THREE is rather good at dressing himself; he shows pride in his own ability. The 3-year-old is often much interested in what he can do to help get dressed, and even more interested in undressing. Undressing is further facilitated by his new ability to unbutton front and side buttons or increased skill with zippers.

Dressing at 3 may include putting on pants, socks, shoes, and, sometimes, sweaters or dresses. Most cannot consistently distinguish back from front or button buttons, though they may try to lace shoes.

But in dressing as well as in eating, things may be worse, rather than better, at 3½. Boy or girl may object to almost every aspect of the dressing process, including the clothes selected. The biggest battle, and the most objection, may relate to anything that needs to be pulled on or off over the head. (Clever mothers soon learn to avoid this type of clothing.) There is even objection to the mere fact of having to get dressed or undressed. This situation, like any other daily routine for the child of this age, can produce a battle.

In other routines these same differences can be observed. THREE's abilities to do for himself are rather good and he is proud to express them. For THREE-AND-A-HALF *any* daily routine sets the stage for the continuing battle which he is waging with his mother for complete control. He wants to do everything *his* way, and *his* way is seldom *her* way.

The most glowing gains for the child of this age come in toileting. Nearly all by 3, certainly by 3½, are now consistently dry, at least in the daytime. (Night wetting in many perfectly normal children often continues till 4 or even 5 or 6 years of age). Bowel training is well established in nearly all except the most perverse.

Perhaps the greatest contrast between 3 and 3½ comes in the realm of emotions. THREE loves to cooperate, either with other children or with his parents. He enjoys the company of other people and for the most part is extremely easy to get along with. His emotions seem stable and secure. He is comfortable with himself and with others.

Unfortunately, at 3½, for all too many, comes the big change. Instead of cooperating, he resists. Instead of doing things your way, he does them his way. Instead of enjoying his mother's company, her very presence all too often seems to stimulate him to his naughtiest mood, his most negative behavior.

Sometimes in fact there seems to be no pleasing him. If you ignore him, he becomes very demanding of your attention. But if you regard him, he will be all too quick with his "Don't look."

Fortunately, perhaps, the 3½-year-old appears to get much comfort from his tensional outlets. Thumb sucking, nail biting, nose picking, hugging a security blanket all can be lifesavers. Also fortunately the child of this age may be fairly amiable and rather good company during playtime when no routines and no special transitions are involved. Also he is often much happier and better behaved with anyone other than his principal caretaker. A baby-sitter or nursery school teacher may indeed find him (or her) quite tractable.

Mothers might take a clue from the fact that their child's chief battle at this age seems to be with them, and plan their days accordingly.


THE 4-YEAR-OLD

We have described (13) the typical 4-year-old as wild and wonderful. Indeed, he or she is definitely both. In our charting of ages of equilibrium and disequilibrium (see Figure 1, page 17), we place the 4-year-old on the side of equilibrium because within himself he seems to be quite secure and comfortable. In fact, adults may feel that he is a little too secure. His sense of self is clearly in very good condition as he boasts and brags and freely tells the world how superior he and his family are, how much he and they can do, and how well he or they can do it.

Grownups in charge may often be disturbed by FOUR's ways, since many at this age do seem to be extremely out-of-bounds, much of the time, in almost every field of behavior.

Motorwise, FOUR often goes definitely out-of-bounds. He sometimes, if angered, hits and spits and kicks. When angry, he may threaten to run away.

Emotionally, he laughs and cries too loudly on even mild provocation.

And his language may be wildest of all. He boasts, he brags, he exaggerates. And all too frequently he ventures into profanity. Any word which he finds gets a rise out of grownups, he uses over and over again.

More than this, he lies. FOUR has discovered that he can bend or even break the truth, and the roof does not fall. Adults may scold, but he knows that he will emerge more or less intact.

## MOTOR BEHAVIOR

Motorwise the typical 4-year-old is rather capable. He now has the balance to stand on one foot for from two to seven seconds. He (or she) can easily walk both up and down stairs with one foot to a step; he can skip (although he still cannot hop). FOUR can catch a beanbag with his hands only, his chest or body no longer involved.

Many now can learn to use roller skates, and some of the better coordinated can even learn to ride a small bicycle if it is equipped with training wheels. FOUR enjoys his new motor abilities and likes to try out physical stunts. In fact, he enjoys almost any sort of athletic activity—to run, to climb, to jump.

He also enjoys his improving motor coordination. He can button large buttons and even lace his shoelaces. He can string even small beads. Many can cut on a line with (child's) scissors. All of these abilities present a challenge which the typical 4-year-old very much enjoys.

## ADAPTIVE BEHAVIOR

In view of his extreme self-confidence and his love of adventure, his willingness to try almost anything, as well as his increasingly mature and effective organism, it is not surprising that the 4-year-old's adaptive behavior goes well beyond that of THREE. He (or she) will try almost anything that comes up and, as often as not, will succeed.

Thus, in an examination situation we observe greatly advanced abilities. At 3½ the child could build a three-cube bridge from a model, but the five-cube gate was beyond him. At 4 girls can imi-

tate the five-cube gate , and at 4½ both sexes can build it from a model, without being shown how.

In drawing, at 3½ the child could do no better than to copy a cross. At 4 he imitates a square, and at 4½ can copy a square from a model. At 4 he (or she) adds on the average five parts to the Incomplete Man, and at 4½ adds seven parts.

FOUR can count, with correct pointing, three objects; FOUR-AND-A-HALF counts four and can answer the question "How many?" He can also print one or two recognizable letters. Some, along toward 4½, can even print their first name. The child is on the threshold of written language.

FOUR can copy the order of a group of things, such as stringing differently colored or differently shaped beads in the order presented in a model. He can also match shapes such as a square, circle, star, in a ten-hole formboard.

Most now enjoy coloring and drawing and many can cut on a line well enough to cut out pictures and then paste them on paper in consecutive order. Or they can cut a picture into parts and then put it together again, puzzle fashion.

Adaptive behavior that also includes language may have reached the point where the child can give likenesses and differences between familiar objects. Or he can tell the biggest and longest of three things and can order five blocks from the heaviest to the lightest, with few mistakes.

As to his playtime, almost anything is of interest. Gross motor play may be his favorite. He loves a jungle gym, a slide, a place to dig, a flat surface on which to ride his tricycle. But even a relatively unequipped yard offers imaginative FOUR a good place to play. Indoors, building with big blocks allows him to exercise both skill and ingenuity. Such blocks are often combined into impressive structures—houses, stores, forts. The child's big muscles seem to want to lift heavy objects. Sometimes FOUR combines his big blocks with trucks and wagons, cars and trains.

Not all of FOUR's play requires materials, indoors or out. His own lively imagination propels him or her through games of house, store, war. Within a short space of time, any group of 4-year-olds may become mother or father, storekeeper, astronaut, doctor, fireman. Doll play remains the most customary kind of imaginative play and is becoming increasingly elaborate.

Dressing up is fun for both boys and girls. Perhaps above all, indoors, children of this age love to be read to. Books they like best portray people or animals in ridiculous actions. FOUR loves to be silly.

Television is becoming of increasing interest and its influence should not necessarily be feared so long as parents continue to supervise and, when possible, to share the viewing.

## LANGUAGE BEHAVIOR

As out-of-bounds as your typical 4-year-old shows himself to be in every field of behavior, it is perhaps in language that this tendency is most conspicuous. As mentioned earlier, the 4-year-old boasts and brags, he prevaricates, he threatens, and above all he or she swears. Parents unaware of the "normalness" of all these behaviors tend to be considerably taken aback at many of the utterances which emerge from the mouths of their presumably "nice" little boys and girls. Friends or even nursery school classmates are all too often blamed, particularly for profanity.

By the age of 4, the average boy or girl has a remarkably large vocabulary. He uses words not only to express his feelings, to accompany his actions, to communicate with friends or adults, but he also uses them to have fun with.

He loves whispering and sharing secrets. He loves shouting and dominating and bossing others around. Best of all he loves to "fool with" language. Nothing pleases him more than silly rhyming. Nothing gives him a bigger kick than to use bathroom talk, especially in the presence of those who show themselves to be disturbed by it.

On the other hand, one of the easiest ways to pull FOUR into line is to confront him with his own kind of language—obvious exaggeration, silly rhyming.

Vocabulary has now increased by leaps and bounds. Some estimate that an average 4-year-old may have as many as 1,550 words at his command. Most FOURS express themselves freely and well. They are now more interested in stories than earlier, will look on when read to, may even ask what certain letters spell.

Sentence structure, grammatical usage, and correctness of tenses are improving. As Laurie and Joseph Braga (21) point out; "Children do not learn to speak by copying adults. They listen to adults, learn the rules, and then make up their own sentences based on the rules they have at the time. They even make mistakes in a systematic way. For instance when beginning to learn the rules for making plurals, children who previously have used the correct plural forms for 'mouse' and 'foot,' now at 4 may say 'mouses' and 'foots.' Later they will learn the exceptions to the rules."

Above all this may be the top "Why?" age. THREES were quick to question, but it sometimes seems that FOUR has a "Why?" for every occasion. He uses the word not only to ask for information but also to ask "Why?" he has to do whatever it is you ask of him. The 4-year-old quite typically accompanies his every action with a running commentary. This is especially noticeable as he makes his own pencil drawing: "This is a big bird. No, it's an airplane. See? It crashes and this is where it's all wrecked up."

In an examination situation the typical FOUR can give his age and the number of his siblings. He can respond correctly to five prepositions by placing a ball on, under, behind, in front of, and in back of a chair. He can repeat three digits correctly in three out of three trials; four correctly in one out of three trials. FOUR frequently uses language to defend his inabilities: "That's hard." "My mommy tells me not to do that." Successes are accompanied by self-praise: "I'm great." "I did that myself, huh?"

By 4½ he can correctly give his own first and last names and also the names of all siblings; he can repeat four digits correctly in two out of three trials.

He can answer correctly all of our usual Comprehension Questions: "What must you do when you are hungry, sleepy, cold?" He can also respond correctly to 16 of the usual Action Agent questions, such as "What scratches, sleeps, flies, bites, etc.?"

Your typical 4-year-old is at home with language and has a great time with it. Articulation in most is no longer infantile.

## PERSONAL-SOCIAL BEHAVIOR

The typical 4-year-old—after the turmoil of 3½—tends to be rather a joy. His enthusiasm, his exuberance, his willingness to go more than half way to meet others in a spirit of fun are all extremely refreshing. In contrast to his difficult, tremulous, insecure 3½-year-old self, the 4-year-old can be a pleasing individual.

With his newfound self-confidence, he does admittedly often challenge the powerful adult, but the tension and anxiety with which he did this six months earlier are gone. FOUR, even when he goes out of bounds—as he so often does—is still an amusing and engaging companion. At least, he gives you half a chance!

He is basically highly positive, enthusiastic, appreciative. This makes him fun to be with, an engaging, amusing, ever-challenging friend. You have to be on your toes to keep up with spirited, fluid, fanciful FOUR, but at least you have an even chance of success. His humor is high, and he appreciates your own. He (or she) can present quite a challenge, but a challenge that is worth it.

Parents and teachers often feel that for all his exuberance, FOUR really appreciates boundaries and rules. He almost seems to welcome someone who can set limits for his almost boundless energy and daring.

With other children, things as a rule go rather well. FOURS enjoy each other; they appreciate the challenge that other children offer. This is an age at which children interest and admire each other most. And children, by what they will and will not accept, often guide the behavior of others.

In a nursery school group there tends to be strong identification with the group. Children like to bring food to share with others. They enjoy inviting other children to their homes to visit them. They love parties and like to celebrate their birthdays, either at home or at school.

FOUR's increasing abilities make home life easier. Most FOURS can feed themselves completely except for cutting, and most can now talk and eat at the same time. Bedtime is now relatively uncomplicated in most. This is an ideal age for the child to change from crib to a big bed. And if the move has not been made earlier, parents can capitalize on it to convince the child that "Now that you are 4 and in your big bed, you won't (whatever he does that they don't like) *any more.*" And chances are that he will believe them.

Toileting is now, for most, an established routine. Many dress and undress themselves without much help, though you may need to lay out clothes for them, each garment correctly oriented since some still have trouble in distinguishing back from front. Some may still have difficulty with buttons though most are surprisingly successful with zippers. Most can get shoes on the correct feet and even lace them. Some can tie a knot in their shoelaces, but cannot yet manage a bow.

Most are also relatively reliable about washing hands and face and brushing teeth.

## FOUR INTO FIVE

For the earlier ages of 2 and 3, it was easy for us to make clear distinctions at the six-months age levels. The normally calm and well-adjusted behavior of TWO quite definitely breaks up at TWO-AND-A-HALF. The same sort of change is easily seen as THREE's calm equilibrium turns into the insecure and difficult behavior so characteristic of THREE-AND-A-HALF.

The changes which seem to occur as FOUR moves into FIVE are of a different nature. Though in our spiral of behavior change, illustrated in Figure 1, we locate the age level of 4½ on the disequilibrium side of the chart, this is not entirely fair to the child of this age.

Actually a more comprehensive view of behavior than we have yet given would include two or perhaps more spirals, instead of one. Instead of merely illustrating the fact that stages of equilibrium alternate with those of disequilibrium as the child grows older, we perhaps should in all fairness include a spiral which shows that growing and changing behavior also alternates between stages of inwardized and outwardized behaviors.

These changes at times match those shown in our original spiral, and sometimes cut across it. What is happening in the age zones 4, 4½, and 5 years seems to be somewhat as follows.

Four is, unquestionably, an age of exuberant expansion. Five is unquestionably a time of calm, temperate, pulled-in, close-to-home behavior.

But the child cannot and does not change from expansive and outgoing FOUR to quiet and inwardized FIVE overnight. The changes occur largely during the second half of the year which comes between the two ages.

It sometimes seems that the child himself does not quite know what to expect. Is he a boisterous, outgoing prankster? Or is he a quiet, demure, home-loving, obedient angel? Only the events of the day will tell.

This not being certain of who or what he is seems, quite naturally, to result in considerable insecurity. The child himself is not quite sure of what he may do, nor is the grownup quite certain either. As pointed out in an earlier publication* (13), a clue to the child's uncertainty is his strong interest in whether or not things are "real."

At 4½, the child does tend to be a bit more self-motivated than he was earlier, and he tends to stay on the job better than he did before. Children of this age are very interested in gathering new information, in perfecting old skills. Play is less wild than at 4, and most are better able to stand frustration. But emotions may be quite un-

*Adapted from Louise B. Ames and Frances L. Ilg, *Your Four Year Old* (New York: Delacorte, 1976).

certain, with laughter and tears following each other in quick succession.

And the child may be less easily shifted than just earlier. It may be harder to distract him with humor than at 4.

At 4½, as the child is becoming aware of authority, a new kind of confused but listening expression, mixed with a bit of fear, crosses his face when a parent reprimands him. For now the awareness of "good" and "bad" things is strengthening. Nothing delights a 4½-year-old more than to hear true stories, either about himself or his parents. He loves stories about how bad his parents were when they were little—and also stories about how good they were.

Prayers, especially spontaneous ones, are welcome at this age and often allay a child's bedtime fears. The thought of God the Father and that He is everywhere can be comforting to some.

All in all, whatever one may say about the child of this age, the opposite may be true since the 4½-year-old is highly unpredictable. But if one keeps in mind where the child has been and where he is going, it can help to define and understand where he is now.


## THE 5-YEAR-OLD

The typical 5-year-old offers an interesting contrast to exuberant FOUR. At 5, a boy or girl tends to be quiet, conforming. For FIVE, mother is the center of the world. He likes to be with her, to please her, to obey. He is most comfortable with the tried and true and definitely prefers to stay within prescribed bounds.

The typical 5-year-old wants to be good, means to be good, and more often than not succeeds in being good. Some mothers even worry that their 5-year-old is "too good." "Today is my lucky day," FIVE will tell you, touchingly. Or, more expansively, "I love everybody in the whole world. Even God." Certainly for the most part, he looks on the bright side of life.

FIVE has little interest in the new and strange. He prefers his own home, own yard, own kindergarten.

One of the major clues to his successful living may be that he is very careful to attempt only what he can achieve. And he usually is a very good judge of his own abilities. He is not smug, but he *is* secure.

Though not expansive in most things, FIVE is expansive intellectually. He loves to be read to, talked to, informed about things he does not know.

## MOTOR BEHAVIOR

FIVE is predictably much more capable than is FOUR. He can skip, using his feet alternately, can walk on tiptoe five steps or more. He can stand on one foot nine seconds or longer, can achieve a broad jump of as much as 27 inches.

In general posture, FIVE is less extreme and less extensor than he was a year earlier. He is more poised and less exuberant. He even stands with arms held near his body.

He loves his tricycle (or small bicycle with training wheels). He climbs with sureness and also enjoys stilts and roller skates or jumping from heights. Jump rope is also coming in as well as acrobatics and trapeze tricks.

Hands as well as whole body are becoming increasingly skilled. He likes to lace his shoes, button buttons, "sew" wool through holes in a card. He likes to place his fingers on the piano keys and strike a chord.

FIVE's economy of movement is in sharp contrast to FOUR's expansiveness of action. The 5-year-old appears more restrained and less active because he maintains one position for longer periods. But though he plays longer in one restricted place, he is a great "helper" who likes to go upstairs to get something for his mother or to go back and forth from kitchen to dining room to put things on the table.

Handedness is often, though not always, well established by 5; and the 5½-year-old can identify the hand he uses for writing. He can usually name his eye, eyebrow, palm, elbow, thumb, and little finger. In block building and other similar activities, he may alternate the use of hands, but the dominant hand is used more frequently. * (14)

By 5½ the average child is even more skillful motorwise. He can stand on one foot for 12 seconds, throw a beanbag overhand, and also catch a beanbag, hands against his chest.

## ADAPTIVE BEHAVIOR

Both motor and adaptive behaviors have now matured to the point where the child relishes a problem-solving situation which in-

*Adapted from Louise B. Ames and Frances L. Ilg, *Your Five Year Old* (New York: Delacorte, 1979).

volves spatial relationships. Increasingly complicated jigsaw puzzles are enjoyed, as well as sewing and carpentry.

In a behavior examination the child can now imitate a three-step set of stairs constructed out of six cubes. He can manage the angle which allows him to copy a fairly good triangle. He attempts a divided rectangle but cannot yet cross the center line, so that his product is likely to end up in a ladder design, even though he may manage to slant the side lines.

He now, on the average, adds eight parts to our Incomplete Man form. Most can print their first name, count ten objects correctly, calculate within five.

By 5½ (or 6) the child can make a four-step set of stairs, using ten cubes. His triangle is now clearly recognizable. In copying the divided rectangle, he may manage to get his side lines across the center vertical dividing line and the outside of his form may now be more rectangular than square. In his effort to complete the Incomplete Man, he now adds eyes which match in size and an arm which matches the printed arm in placement and upward slant.

FIVE can print not only his first name, but also the first letter of his last name, write two or three numbers recognizably, count 12 objects correctly.

The adaptive abilities of the typical FIVE fit well into the usual (nonacademic) kindergarten routine. He loves to cut, trace, draw, paste, string beads, and make things out of small pieces of paper or cloth.

Block play is still a favorite of both sexes. Girls build houses for their dolls. Boys are more likely to build roads, tracks, bridges, tunnels, trucks, planes, fire engines. Both sexes like to build big houses with big blocks or to make tent houses out of chairs and blankets.

## LANGUAGE BEHAVIOR

Five may be a quiet age in many respects, but it is a time when language blossoms. FIVE loves to talk. And he is much more grown-up in his language than at 4. He for the most part talks entirely without so-called "infantile articulation." His answers to questions are more succinct and to the point than just earlier. His own questions are fewer and more relevant. He asks questions for information, not merely for social intercourse or for practice in the art of speaking. Since his questions now betray an interest in the practical workings of the universe, his "Why?" and "What for?" questions are recognized as no longer just a stall; thus, they are not as trying to the adult as they have been earlier.

The typical 5-year-old likes to talk. In fact some mothers complain that their child talks constantly—that it is impossible to get away from the sound of his voice. Up to a point, conversation is welcomed and even relished. But admittedly some children do talk too much. In fact this may be one of the kindergartner's problems. It is hard for him to inhibit his constant conversation.

Language is now extremely meaningful to the child for its own sake. He likes new words, big words. He likes to ask, "What does . . . spell?" Most are excited about the idea that they themselves soon will be able to read.

Our own publications on school readiness in general and reading readiness in particular emphasize that it should be the child's behavior age and not his chronological age which determines not only the time of school entrance but most especially the time when reading instruction should be introduced.

Some natural-born early readers may well be reading spontaneously by 5 or even earlier. Many other children would do much better if reading were delayed till they were fully 6 or even 7. The introduction of reading instruction before the child is developmentally ready tends to lead to confusion and failure.

Then "remedial reading" instruction enters the picture. The child who has gone through the sequence—too early reading instruction/failure/remediation—will in all likelihood not be as successful at reading or as enthusiastic or confident about it as the one who has been permitted to wait to begin at his own good time.

According to the much-quoted Piaget, the child is now still in the "preoperational" stage of thinking. He knows that words represent objects and ideas. He learns that actions have both causes and effects—that is, pushing a switch makes a light go on. But he may still explain outside events in terms of his own wishes and needs: "It rained because I wanted it to." He may even believe that objects and natural events have human thoughts and feelings: "It rained because the cloud was angry."

In other words, children still have some difficulty, as earlier at 4½, in distinguishing between fantasy and reality. "It happened by magic" is still an acceptable answer to a child's question (from his point of view).

However, the 5-year-old is beginning to try to figure things out for himself. He makes his own generalizations, often based on inadequate evidence. Thus, if both of his grandfathers die before his grandmothers do, he may ask, "Do Daddies die first?" Or if by chance he has been told that two certain brown dogs are females and two black ones males, he may conclude that all brown dogs are females and all black ones males.

Concept of number, up through ten, is usually well established. Also FIVE can define familiar objects in terms of use. In the examination situation he can give his first and last names, answer correctly two of the Comprehension B questions—"What must you do when you have lost something?" and "What must you do before you cross the street?" He can answer correctly 17 Action Agent questions and can identify correctly 15 of the Picture Vocabulary objects.

Though most children have loved being read to ever since 2 years of age, for many this form of entertainment reaches a peak at 5. In fact there may be nothing a 5-year-old likes better than being read to, even though he enjoys spending considerable time looking at books by himself, picking out words he knows or even, in some cases, doing a little actual reading on his own.

FIVES still enjoy the humorous, silly, ridiculous books which were favorites at 4, books like Benton's *Don't Ever Wish for a Seven-Foot Bear*. They are especially fond of books about animals that act like people, such as Duvoisin's *The Crocodile in the Tree,* or *Petunia's Treasure*. Or they like books which help them develop their increasing intellectual understanding, such as Hafter's *Colors* or his *Yes and No: A Book of Opposites*.

Verbally FIVE is not as humorous as he was just earlier. He may be too mature for the silly verbal humor which so delighted him at 4. Some FIVES most-enjoyed humor may come in relation to their pretending not to be obedient. FIVE may make jokes to the effect that he is not going to do what his parents tell him to.

But flashes of humor can be seen in the child's own spontaneous stories: "Once there was a Pontiac. It was crazy. It was going down the road with no one in it." Or the incongruous as well as the ridiculous tickles his sense of humor.

## PERSONAL-SOCIAL BEHAVIOR

FIVE is, to the adult, tremendously appealing with his serious air. He is impressed with his own growing ability to assume little responsibilities and to imitate grown-up behavior. He is very proud when parent or teacher compliments something he has accomplished.

To the child of this age his parents, especially his mother, are the center of the world, and he likes nothing better than to be with them and to do "good" things which will please them.

Relationship with siblings is improving somewhat over what it was earlier. Many FIVES play reasonably well with older siblings. And some girls are regular little mothers to their younger sibs. However, FIVE often gets on best with children outside his immediate family, especially those of his own age. With his natural desire to please and to have things go smoothly, he is a much easier playmate than he was at 4 or than he will be at 6.

However, even the friendly 5-year-old does sometimes encounter a child with whom he just cannot get along. Whose fault this is is not the question. Since FIVE, with his gentleness and good will, tends to be quite vulnerable socially, he should be protected from any overaggressive or incompatible friend.

As to home routines, FIVE feeds himself very adequately, and appetite is now usually quite good. But his manners may still fall far short of adult standards. He may dawdle as he eats, talk too much, wriggle in his chair. But most need very little help with eating unless they tire toward the end of a meal. Most can now use a knife even though they cannot cut meat.

Food preferences are still rather marked. FIVE likes plain, simple cooking. Gravies, casseroles, puddings, cooked root vegetables, anything complicated or with a strong taste may be refused. The child especially dislikes stringy, lumpy foods.

Bedtime for most becomes an increasingly easy time. They like to have stories read to them, either in the living room or after they reach their bedroom. Getting ready for bed usually goes smoothly. Many still take a toy animal or doll to bed with them. If they don't go to sleep quickly and easily, some like to "read" to themselves. Still others lie quietly in the dark, singing or talking to themselves.

A few still need to get up frequently for a drink, something to eat, or to go to the bathroom, but most can take care of their own needs without bothering parents.

However, unfortunately, the 5-year-old is a good example of what we describe as "good days and bad nights." Frightening dreams are frequent, and the child may awaken crying or screaming. Usually it is hard for him to tell much about what he dreamed, but fortunately most can be comforted rather easily and quickly.

Toileting presents few problems and some may even be dry at night. As to dressing themselves, this is an age when mothers report, "He can, but he doesn't." Most do have the abilities needed, except for tying shoelaces or buttoning difficult buttons, but may not use the abilities they have. They can do what is needed, so for many the challenge is gone and they may demand more help than they asked for earlier. Undressing is still definitely easier than dressing.

## THE TRANSITION FROM 5 TO 6

In general the typical 5-year-old tends to be a creature of joy, a very pleasant member of the household. Things change, for many, at 6. In fact the beginnings of a definite change for the worse are all too often evident around 5½ years of age.

At 5 Mother was the center of the young person's world. At 6 he is the center of his own world. He wants to be first, to be loved best, to have the most of everything. And especially to have his own way! "Brash," "combative" are words that mothers often use in describing him (or her).

FIVE-AND-A-HALF is all too characteristically hesitant, dawdling, indecisive—or, at the opposite pole, overdemanding and explosive. Behavior is, discouragingly, often characterized by the opposite extremes which we saw earlier at 2½ years of age; that is, the child may be extremely shy and then the next minute very bold, extremely affectionate and then almost without warning highly antagonistic. And when he does not have the courage to defy you outright, he dawdles—which amounts to much the same thing. Whatever you want him to do very often does not get done.

*Emotionally* the child of this age may seem to be in an almost constant state of tension, though fortunately most are calmer at school than at home. Emotionally the child finds it hard to conclude an explosion or sulk or burst of tears once it has begun. This may be the beginnings once again of a tantrum age.

*Physically* too we see signs of a breakup. The almost predictably healthy 5-year-old now suddenly has many colds, headaches, earaches, stomachaches. Or his feet hurt, his face hurts. He may even revert to toileting accidents when overexcited. And physically rather placid FIVE has now reached a point where there is an increase of tensional outlets—many hand-to-mouth gestures; chewing, biting, or tapping a pencil; chewing at a collar or any other piece of loose clothing.

*Motorwise* there is more restlessness, less composure than we saw at 5. Pencil grasp may be awkward and there may be frequent change of grasp. Though he may not, as at 6, "trip over a piece of string," his total body seems less under control than just earlier. And it becomes increasingly difficult for him to sit still for long periods.

All in all, organization is breaking up, reality often is being shattered. And in a way he enjoys all this upheaval. Thus a child of this age may voluntarily cross his eyes when he does not understand something, when he is surprised, or when he wants to be silly.

Even the child's *teeth* are breaking up, so to speak. One by one those even, pearly baby teeth are starting to loosen, beginning at about this age, with the lower incisors.

Unfortunately, any smooth stage of behavior, like the one seen at 5, must break up before the child can reach a higher, more mature stage of equilibrium. Thus the typical 6-year-old resembles a 5½-year-old at his worst. But that higher and more mature stage does come in most children somewhere around 6½ years of age, a splendid time of equilibrium for many.


## THE 6-YEAR-OLD

SIX is indeed a paradox. Like his younger 2½-year-old self, he lives at opposite extremes, and whatever he does he does the opposite just as readily. In fact the mere choice of chocolate may trigger an overpowering need for vanilla.

"Six is a hard age to be" confided one little boy to his mother— hard for him and hard for those around him.

In many ways he is a delight. His enthusiasm, his naïveté, his fresh approach to the new and different make the 6-year-old first-grader a pleasant person to be with. That is, until something does not suit him. Then, in a moment, sunshine is indeed followed by shadow. SIX is also stubborn. He has considerable difficulty in making up his mind, but once made up, it is hard to change it.

One of SIX's biggest problems may be his relationship to his mother. Whereas at 5, Mother was the center of his world, the child himself is now the center of his own world and he wants things to go *his* way. He wants to be first and best. He wants to win.

Whereas at 5 obedience came almost automatically, now it seems very hard for the child to do what his mother wants him to do. Many is the tangle, only to be resolved at bedtime, when he asks his mother, "Have I been a good boy today?" He loves his mother, but at the same time he is trying to gain independence from her.

Things often go so badly around the house that, as one mother put it, "Every day I get up with the solemn promise to myself to try and make my daughter feel loved. But then she does some impossible thing and I scold and off we go, bad as ever!"

The child is, at least part of the time, demanding and difficult because he is still quite insecure and his emotional needs are very great. Only much patience and love on the part of his parents can serve to meet his needs. But if they can be met, he can be not only sunny and sharing but also giving.

Also he can be enthusiastic and emotionally warm. These are among his dearest and most engaging characteristics. There is nobody quite like a lively 6-year-old—when things go well!

## MOTOR BEHAVIOR

Even by 5½, and more so at 6, the poise and motor equilibrium so characteristic of 5 are breaking down. True, the child's motor abilities are actually increasing, but so is his restlessness. It seems that he is constantly on the go, lugging, tugging, digging, dancing, climbing, pushing, pulling.

The outdoor world tends to provide opportunities for release of this sheer physical energy, but indoors things do not always go as well. Awkwardness and misplaced energy often result in accidents. In fact, poise may have departed to the point where a mother remarks, "Seems as if he could trip over a piece of string."

Even eye-hand behavior may now give difficulty. There is a certain awkwardness apparent as the child performs fine motor tasks, even though he has an increased demand for such activities. In carpentry, for instance, he may need a good deal of help (more than he will accept). He pounds and pounds in driving nails, but often fails to hit them on the head and may even break the board. His saw bends and gets jammed. Scissors may cut other than the cloth or paper they were intended to cut. Life is not always easy!

SIX seems to be consciously balancing his body in space. He is everywhere—climbing trees, crawling over, under, and about his large block structures. He seems to be all legs and arms as he dances about a room, and his coordination is all too often faulty.

Just to observe him may be quite fatiguing to the peace-loving adult. True, his abilities with jump rope or swing or bicycle may be rather impressive, but he tends to overextend himself. He swings too high. He builds his block tower too tall. He attempts constructions which exceed his very real ability. And even when sitting, SIX may be constantly active and very wiggly. In fact, even his mouth is busy, as he extends his tongue, bites his lips, chews his pencil. Clearly, he has energy to spare.

### ADAPTIVE BEHAVIOR

Just watch a 6-year-old attack first-grade tasks and you will marvel at the extent of his or her abilities. He loves to color, cut and paint and paste. He loves to draw—people, houses, boats and trains and spaceships. He loves to make things, of paper, cardboard, wood. He loves to build with blocks, large and small. Even mud and water can be used constructively.

In coloring or printing, enthusiasm may exceed execution. Often eye-hand coordination is awkward as is grasp of crayon or pencil. The child may stand and lean way over the table, or he may rest his head on his arm as he works at drawing or printing.

The typical 6-year-old, at the beginning of both reading and writing, loves to print, or at least to struggle with printing. Grasping his pencil awkwardly near the tip, tongue often protruding with his effort, he struggles with numbers and letters. Nearly all SIXES can print their numbers from 1 to 11, and nearly half can go all the way to 20. Girls at 6, boys at 6½, can print both their first and last names. Letters and numbers, however, are often reversed, and both tend to be large, labored, and uneven.

The child of this age often seems to be more interested in process (what he is doing at the moment) than in his final product. In building a tower of cubes, for instance, he makes a more deliberate, careful approach than earlier, trying very hard to place each cube with accuracy. The result may be a less good alignment than he managed when he was 5. Things are breaking up and changing for him, visually as in other respects.

The behavior examination gives SIX the opportunity to demonstrate some of his newfound powers and abilities. Cube behavior reaches a pinnacle of ten cube steps built, with or even without demonstration, by both girls and boys. In copying a divided rectangle, for the first time, SIX has the three lines (horizontal and two angled) cross the center vertical line. Diamonds are approaching an adequate shape. And now an average of nine parts are added to the Incomplete Man figure, with an accurate completion of the area at the neck.

SIX's adaptive behavior is indeed far beyond that of his earlier 5-year-old self, but it still has a way to go.

## LANGUAGE BEHAVIOR

Your typical 6-year-old likes to talk, and talk, and talk. Sometimes even his ever-loving mother may wish that he did not talk quite so much. But he so dotes on conversation, so loves to share his thoughts!

Most girls and boys now have rather good pronunciation, and their grammatical construction tends to be rather accurate. In fact, most can detect their own mistakes, or even when they cannot, will accept correction.

In an examination situation, SIX is on the verge of being able to tell the day and month of his birthday. (This ability becomes normative at 6½.) He can repeat five digits in one of three trials and can respond correctly to 16 pictures in our picture vocabulary test; he can answer correctly 19 Action Agent questions, such as "What flies?" "What swims?" "What roars?"

SIX can also differentiate morning and afternoon, identify his left hand and his right.

The child of this age not only has much information to share, he also has great curiosity. His questions, about things both mundane and otherworldly, seem endless. A few may talk so fast that they stutter, but for most this is transitory and should not be considered worrisome. SIX likes to use new words, enjoys the excitement of mastering big words. Some are already very good on the telephone.

The child of 6 is often much interested in the language of arithmetic. Most can recite their numbers up to 30, and like to have either Mother or Father pose simple questions in arithmetic for them to answer.

Many of the table games which SIX so loves, such as anagrams, dominoes, and simple card games that demand matching, fit in well with his intellectual interests. Those games which involve throwing dice and advancing counters on a board give exercise to his mathematical abilities.

Reading, whether being read to or spelling out letters for himself, is now an all-engrossing interest. SIX in school, especially as the year goes on, can usually accomplish a creditable amount of reading. He is learning to read not only single words but also combinations of words. He can usually recognize a word even out of its familiar context. Many now need a marker or to use their fingers as they read. This of course should be permitted; otherwise they are all too likely to lose their place.

### PERSONAL-SOCIAL BEHAVIOR

Your 6-year-old, as we have said, is a lively, lovely creature, dynamic, energetic, and enthusiastic, but one whose life is not without complications. His biggest problem may be his two-way nature, which swings him so swiftly between opposite poles of conduct; he may be beautiful and bubbly one minute, but difficult and quarrelsome the next.

His greatest personal difficulties may be with his mother. He is characteristically "all mixed up with her." He loves her, depends on her, needs her, and yet when things go wrong, he takes his frustrations out on her. He seeks and so very much wants to be praised, but unfortunately his behavior is often such that praise is hard to give.

Things tend to go better with his father, whom he admires but somewhat fears, or with his teacher, whom he respects, but with whom he tends to be much less involved than with his mother.

Relations with siblings and friends are variable. His biggest problem may be that he cannot stand to lose when playing competitively; he even cheats or breaks up the game if he finds himself losing. And he is extremely jealous. He watches with an eagle eye to be sure that somebody else (especially a sibling) does not get a bigger piece of cake or does not get an extra turn.

SIX's need to come out ahead, to be first, to have the most of everything, unfortunately often leads to petty pilfering. He is also not above frequent departures from the truth. And, if asked if he is the one who broke the lamp or spilled the perfume, he is almost certain to deny his guilt.

Mealtimes with the family may cause much difficulty since SIX, in his superactive way, tends to fidget and spill and reach across the table and chew with his mouth open. He will very likely knock over his milk and it is not too unusual for him to fall right out of his chair onto the floor.

Dressing, too, can bring its problems. As just earlier, mothers say, "He can, but he won't." And girls, especially, tend to have great difficulty on school days in deciding which outfit to wear.

Bedtime, especially if Mother has time to chat and listen, is vastly improved over what it was when boy or girl was younger. A good, long bedtime chatting period can do wonders to smooth out the tangles of the day.

SIX can be a delightful companion, a marvel of spontaneity and enthusiasm, all big smiles and big hugs; but he can also be a difficult companion, because of his own personal tangles which so quickly enmesh the key people in his life.

Fortunately, as growth continues its predictable swings between outwardized and inwardized behavior, between equilibrium and disequilibrium, a few more months bring the child to the customarily calm and comfortable age of 6½. On the way toward the inwardization of 7, too-far-out SIX calms down, quiets down, takes life easier, finds that his interpersonal relationships are easier and more rewarding.

The age period of 6½ tends to emphasize most of the positive aspects of 6 with few of its difficulties. It is an age worth waiting for.

# PART TWO

# 4

## Motor Behavior

In the early months of life, particularly before a child can speak, motor tests are perhaps the most revealing of all the Gesell behavior tests. They offer almost an embarrassment of riches. Each of the four basic postures—supine, prone, sitting, and standing—provides a situation which must be mastered by the child.

In prone behavior alone we have identified 22 separate and specific stages which the child must traverse before he is ready to stand and walk (34).

By 2 years of age, the usual boy or girl has mastered basic skills needed in all four of these postures. He no longer spends much time supine unless he sleeps on his back. Long since, he has acquired the ability to sit unsupported, to creep, to pull to stand, to stand and walk.

Now comes the perfecting and elaboration of postural control. These accomplishments are important but less striking than what has gone before. And since we divided motor behavior into gross motor and fine motor, we soon come to the place where many of the so-called fine motor behaviors are literally identical with what we call adaptive behaviors. Thus in our Behavior Schedule they are for the most part listed under *both* motor and adaptive behavior.

Actually the relative predominance of motor tests in the early years has raised some questions which have never been fully answered. Though not everyone agrees, we ourselves believe that infant tests are to quite an extent predictive of later behavior. In fact, our own research (2) suggests that the child who is advanced in behavior in infancy continues to be advanced not only on behavior tests but on intelligence tests as well.

However, we have always emphasized that a child's relative ratings in the four major fields of behavior—motor, adaptive, language, and personal-social—are fully as important as the *average* of all his behaviors. Thus, it may be admitted that an advancement in motor behavior does not guarantee advancement in the other fields.

In fact, the relative early advancement in infancy of native African babies or of blacks in the United States, due to their advanced early motor behavior, has been noted (49). It has also been observed that such children often rate lower as they grow older due to the increased weight of adaptive and language items in most test batteries.

There are those who believe that early training and practice can increase or improve the young child's behavior to a remarkable degree. The latest exposition of this notion is found in *Kindergarten Is Too Late* by Masaru Ibuka (41). The reader is referred to this book as an excellent example of a point of view which is diametrically opposed to our own belief that Nature takes its time and that behavior cannot be substantially speeded up by training or practice.

At any rate, whatever the age, we consider motor tests an important part of any preschool battery.

As the child carries out any of the individual motor tasks which we include, he demonstrates not only the level of his neuromotor organization but also the quality of his behavior. The examiner should observe not only the age-appropriateness or inappropriateness of the behavior exhibited, but also the way in which the child performs the individual tasks. Often a child is able to carry out a task in a manner which earns him or her a plus score, but the quality of behavior reveals a lingering immaturity or awkwardness.

Laterality patterns offer additional information. These patterns can be observed through the child's hand preference in picking up pellets, completing puzzles, or throwing an object, as well as in copying forms or building with cubes. Also such situations as standing on one foot, hopping, and skipping give good clues as to foot preference. Unusual hand tremors or loss of spatial orientation during gross motor tasks should also be recorded.

A few of the motor items included in our Behavior Schedule, for instance, "Rides tricycle using pedals at 3 years" are as a rule best checked by asking the parent about home behavior. This item is seldom included in the actual conduct of the examination.

Whether or not the child walks up and down stairs alone (2

years) or alternates feet in going up stairs (3 years) can be observed casually at the time of the examination if stairs are available. Otherwise, once again, a parent's reporting must be relied upon.

Whether or not the child can kick a large ball without demonstration is discussed here along with other motor tests, but it is not included in our recording sheet since it is normative at 2 years of age, an age younger than that at which present subjects were tested.

All cube situations, though they are included in our Behavior Schedules under both motor and adaptive behaviors, are described in Chapter 5, "Adaptive Behavior."

However, Pellets into Bottle, though they, too, are included under both motor and adaptive behavior in our schedules, since they involve probably a greater element of fine motor than adaptive expertness, are described in the present chapter on "Motor Behavior."

Except for Pellets into Bottle which may be given, depending on the examiner's preference, fairly early in the examination, the motor tests are often given at the end of the examination after table-top situations have been completed. The child is encouraged to stand up, and table and chair are pushed to one side. (Responses to all motor tests are recorded on the recording sheet. Examiner will need a silent stopwatch for timed items and a tape measure or yardstick.)

Motor tests proceed as follows:

### PELLETS INTO BOTTLE

*Material:* Examiner—A silent stopwatch. Motor recording sheet. Child—Ten pellets 8 mm. in diameter, flat on one side and convex on the other. A glass bottle 7 cm. in height and 2 cm. in diameter at the opening.

*Procedure:* Place pellets in a row beside the bottle, on the side of the child's preferred hand. Say, "Put them all into the bottle, *just one at a time.*" Start the stopwatch.

If the child tries to pick up more than one at a time, restrain his hand. Say, "Just one at a time," "Now another," etc.

After completion, dump out the pellets and arrange them on the opposite side of the bottle. Say, "Now use this *other* hand. Just one at a time." Start the stopwatch as the first pellet plinks into the bottle. If the child starts to change hands, say, "Remember, you are using *this* hand now."

*Recording:* Record the time needed by the child to put the pellets into the bottle. Record time needed to complete the task with the right hand and with the left hand separately.

## KICKS LARGE BALL

*Material:* Large ball. White rubber, red and green stripes encircling middle. Diameter 6 cm. (SR 4526, Seamless Rubber Company, New Haven, Connecticut 06511.)

*Procedure:* Put the ball on the floor immediately in front of the child's feet, the child having first been led to the center of the room away from available supports. Say, "Kick the ball, give it a big kick," or, if necessary, "Kick it with your foot." Even touch both of his shoes if he does not understand the instructions. If need be, demonstrate, but if demonstration is necessary, the test is not considered as passed at the 2-year-old level.

*Recording:* On recording sheet, check either succeeds or fails.

## WALKS ON TIPTOE

*Procedure:* Ask, "Can you walk on your toes?" Emphasize "Tiptoe" if need be. Say, "Try it, like this." Examiner demonstrates.

*Recording:* Then check on the recording sheet the item that describes the way the task was completed. Choices indicated are:
Attempts to walk on tiptoe with/without hand held
Takes 2–3 steps with/without hand held
Takes_____steps with/without hand held

## SKIPS

*Procedure:* Ask, "Can you skip like this?" Examiner demonstrates. If child says, "No," say, "Show me how you would try."

*Recording:* Check on the recording sheet the item that describes the way the task was completed. Choices are:
On one foot
On alternating feet

## JUMPS IN PLACE

*Procedure:* Say, "Can you jump? Show me how you can jump." Demonstrate simple jump, straight up.

*Recording:* Check on the recording sheet the item that describes the way the task was completed:

Attempts
Both feet leave the floor

### JUMPS DOWN

*Procedure:* Take child to bottom step of a staircase or to a platform 8–9
inches high. (Or a low chair may be used so long as the examiner se-
cures it tightly when the child jumps.) Say, "Show me how you jump
down." Offer hand if necessary on first try. Then ask child to repeat
without a helping hand on the second try if it appears that he might be
able to succeed.

*Recording:* Check the item on score sheet that best describes the way the
child completed the task. Choices are:
    Attempts, but steps, or other body parts touch floor
    Lands on feet
    Lands on toes

### STANDS ON ONE FOOT

*Procedure:* Take the child to an area of the room without furniture or other supports. Say, "Show me how you can stand on one foot, like this,
while I count." Demonstrate. As soon as the child picks up one foot, begin a slow count, out loud, one number to a second, and continue until
child's lifted foot touches the ground, or the child leans on something.
Offer a hand if necessary, but encourage the child to try alone after
that.
    Give three tries for each foot if the count remains below ten. Except
for youngest children, use a stopwatch as well as counting.

*Recording:* Check on recording sheet the item that describes the way the
child stands on one foot. Choices are:
    Attempts with/without hand held
    Momentary balance
    Balance of 1–2 seconds
    Balance of 4–8 seconds
    Balance of more than 8 seconds

### STANDING BROAD JUMP

*Procedure:* Take the child to the beginning of the tape measure which has
been placed on the floor. Say, "Show me how far you can jump—can
you jump right up to here?" (Indicate a point about 36" to 40" from the
beginning of the tape.) Encourage a two-footed broad jump but accept
anything beyond a step. Both feet must be off the ground at the same

time sometime during the activity, but takeoff and landing need not involve use of both feet simultaneously. Allow three tries and score the best performance.

*Recording:* Record the broad jump according to success or failure. Record with a check mark (✔) if the child succeeds. If he does not, record with a comment in the space allotted for Standing Broad Jump.

## Hops on One Foot

*Procedure:* Demonstrate hopping forward on one foot. Then say, "Show me how far you can hop along here," indicating a 6-foot tape which has been laid on the floor. Add, "Can you go all the way to the end?"

*Recording:* Check on the recording sheet the item that describes the way the task was completed. Choices are:
Hops with both feet off the ground
Hops on one foot

## Throwing and Catching

*Material:* A rectangular bean bag 4½ inches by 2½ inches. A wooden "performance" box, 15½" tall, with a 10" by 7" opening at the top.

*A1. Beanbag—Spontaneous Throw*
Hand the child a beanbag. Then stand 6 feet from the child and say, "Throw it to me." Give three trials.
Check the item on the recording sheet that describes the child's best performance. Possibilities are:
Aim far off, uncatchable
Aim fair, barely catchable
Aim good, between knees and head, easy arm reach
Aim right at examiner's trunk

*A2. Beanbag, Overhand Throw Requested (Only If A1 Is Failed)*
Demonstrate by holding the beanbag next to your ear. (If the child is left-handed, demonstrate with your right hand; if he is right-handed, use your left.) Say, "Throw it from up here."
Check the item on the recording sheet that describes the child's performance. Items are:

Stance:   Child faces frontward
Child advances wrong foot (same side as throwing arm)
Child advances right foot (opposite side from arm)

Arm:    Hand off to side
Hand over shoulder, elbow forward
Hand over shoulder, elbow back or sideways

Aim:    Far off, uncatchable
Fair, barely catchable
Good, between knees and head, easy arm reach
Right at examiner's trunk

## B. Beanbag Throw for Accuracy

Put performance box on the floor, open end up, 6 feet from child. Say, "Now throw the bag into the box." Give three tries.

Check the item on the recording sheet that describes the child's performance. Circle the number of times the bag hits or enters the box. Items to be checked or circled are:

Misses box on all three tries
Hits box outside—1   2   3
Gets bag into box—1   2   3

## C. Beanbag Catch

Stand 6 feet from the child and throw the bag to him underhanded, right to his chest, saying as you do so, "Catch the bag." Give three tries. Do not count the examiner's poor shots, if any.

Check on the recording sheet the item that describes the child's performance:

Any method
Hands vs. chest or better
Hands only

## Motor—Recording Sheet

Name_____

Age_____

Pellets
_____ sec. with right
_____ sec. with left

Walk on tiptoe
Attempts with/without hand held
Takes 2-3 steps with/without hand held
Takes _____ steps without hand held

Skip
On one foot
On alternating feet

Jump in place
Attempts
Both feet leave the floor

Jump down
Attempts but steps, or other body parts touch floor
Lands on feet
Lands on toes

Stands on one foot
Attempts with/without hand held
Momentary balance
Balance of 1-2 seconds
Balance of 4-8 seconds
Balance of more than 8 seconds

Jumps
Standing broad jump

Hops on one foot
Hops with both feet off the ground
Hops on one foot

Beanbag Throw
Throws underhand
Throws overhand
Advanced throwing (advances—with opposite foot)

Beanbag Catch
Attemps but misses
Catches with arms against chest
Catches with hands against chest
Catches with hands alone

Normative data for all of these motor tests will be found in Chapter 8, "Behavior Norms," and also in Chapter 9, "Behavior Schedules."

# 5

## Adaptive Behavior

Adaptive behavior is of special importance because, with the possible exception of language, it is the area which often interests parents as well as examiners most.

That first step, that first word are of course of supreme importance, but by the time the child is 2 years of age they are far in the past. Now comes the time when what most people think of as the "mind" begins to express itself.

Actually we do not make a special distinction between mind and body. As Dr. Gesell so often remarked, "Mind manifests itself in whatever the infant and child may do." Thus to us gross motor behavior is as much an expression of the mind in action as is manipulation of objects or spoken words.

At any rate the child's adaptive behavior during the years covered in this volume is easy to elicit and to observe and of great importance in telling us how far the child's mind and body in action have developed.

Adaptive behavior has another special advantage. Possibly more than language behavior tests, tests of adaptive behavior are relatively culture fair and culture free. Assuming that he or she has had any experience whatsoever with blocks or with crayon and paper, a child from a culturally disadvantaged home should not be at any special disadvantage in responding to the kinds of test situations which we present under the category of adaptive behavior.

Another special advantage of our adaptive behavior tests is that even the child who is not signally successful in responding at or near his or her age level need not be aware of this failure. Thus at the age of 2½, the normative expectation is that a child will build a tower of ten cubes. However, the child who makes a tower of only four or five, if sufficiently praised by the examiner, will in all probability feel success. The child who adds a too long and too low arm to the Incomplete Man, unless somebody points this out to him, will most likely consider that he has added a satisfactory arm.


## CUBE BEHAVIOR

Block play is an almost universal interest of the preschool child. When only 36 weeks old, the infant usually can combine two cubes in pat-a-cake fashion. At one year or just after, he places one cube over another, and around 15 months he actually builds a tower of two. Each added few months adds another block to his or her tower till around 2½ years of age when the "average" child can build a tower of ten. And then as the years go by, with or without demonstration, he can build a train, a bridge, a gate, and finally steps.

It is important to note that the child's own drive, quite as much as the directions given by the examiner, produce his block-building behavior. Blocks or cubes have a natural appeal to almost all children and easily activate their interest. It is the exceptional child who does not respond positively to them.

Since this is usually the first formal test situation presented, the child should not be hurried into the activity, but rather should be given ample time to explore and to make his own adjustment.

The series of cube tests employs ten one-inch red cubes and begins with an observation of the child's spontaneous play with the cubes. Following this he is asked to build a vertical tower, a train, a bridge, a gate, and (first) a six-cube and (later) a ten-cube steps.

There is a wealth of information to be obtained from the child's responses to these several cube situations. Among the many things revealed are: ability in constructive block play, ability to understand and follow directions, the presence of any noticeable hand tremor, the level of fine motor skills, the length of attention span, and the level of functioning in a structured task in contrast to self-motivated building play.

*Material:* Examiner—Recording sheet. Child—An 8½-by-11-inch sheet of green paper and ten red one-inch square cubes.

*General Directions:* The cubes are presented in formation on the sheet of green paper. Nine cubes form a square, with the tenth cube on top of the middle one. The paper is placed horizontally, near the edge of the examination table, in front of the child's chair.

Examiner continues presenting tasks until the child fails after being given a demonstration. The train is given only to children up to 3 years of age or to older children who fail the bridge. Children of 3 and older are given the bridge immediately after they have finished the tower.

*Procedure:*    1. SPONTANEOUS BLOCK PLAY:

Say, "Build something—anything you like." As the child works, ask, "What are you making?" When he is finished, ask, "What did you make?"

2. TOWER BUILDING:

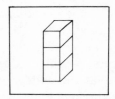

Say, "See" or "Look" and build a tower of three cubes. Then say, "Now see how high you can build it," indicating that the child should add blocks to the examiner's tower of three. If the tower falls before all ten are in place, give a second trial.

   3. TRAIN:

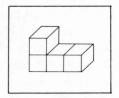

(This item is given to children 3 years of age or younger and to older children who fail the bridge.) *Build this* as well as the more difficult items when they need to be demonstrated *well out of the child's reach.* If the child grabs for the model, say, "This one is mine. You build yours over there."

Say, "Look" or "See" or "Watch." Then align three cubes in a row, saying, "One car, two cars, three cars." Put the fourth cube on top of the first and say, "And this is the chimney." Push the train across the table, saying, "See, the train goes choo-choo-choo." Leave the model standing and push four other cubes toward the child. Say, "You make one."

If a second demonstration is needed, rebuild the train, saying, "One, two, three, and the chimney goes on top."

If the child of 3 years or younger successfully completes the train, go on to the bridge, using the testing folder for a screen. If the child had difficulty with the train, build the bridge without the screen so that he can see what you are doing.

4. BRIDGE:

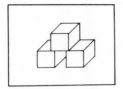

(Use testing folder as a screen.) Say, "I'm going to build something, and when it is finished I'll show it to you." Build a three-cube bridge behind the screen. When finished, remove the screen and ask, "What does that look like to you?" Accept any response given.

If there is no response, ask, "Does it look like a bridge?" ("Or tunnel?"), leave the model up and give the child three cubes. Say, "You make one just like this."

If the child fails to build the bridge, demonstrate without the screen so that he can see what you are doing.

If the child needs a demonstration and even then fails to imitate, accept his failure and discontinue the cube situations. If he succeeds in making a bridge, either with or without demonstration, go on to the gate.

5. GATE:

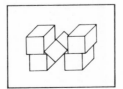

(Use a screen.) Say, "I'm going to build something else, and when it's finished I'll show it to you." Build a five-cube gate behind the screen. When finished, remove the screen. Ask, "What does it look like to you?" Accept any response given. If there is no verbal response, say, "You make one just like this."

If a demonstration is needed, rebuild the gate without the screen so that the child can see what you are doing.

If the child needs a demonstration and still fails to imitate, accept his product, and discontinue the cubes. If he succeeds, either with or without demonstration, try the steps.

### 6. SIX-CUBE STEPS:

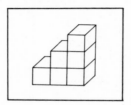

(Use a screen.) Say, "I'm going to build something else." Build the six-cube steps behind the screen. When finished, remove the screen and ask, "What does it look like to you?" Accept any response given. If there is no response, point to the top, middle, and bottom cubes in order and say, "Down, down, down; it could be steps, couldn't it?"

Do not leave the model standing, but say, "Take a good look. I'm going to knock this down and you can build it up again. Ready?"

Give the child the cubes used for the model and say, "Now you build———" (whatever he has named the structure). If a demonstration is needed, omit the screen and build with the child watching, saying, "Watch how I do it." Build vertically with three cubes in the first column, two in the second, and one in the last. As the child looks at the steps, the highest column should be at his right.

### 7. TEN-CUBE STEPS:

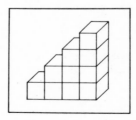

If the child needs a demonstration and still fails to imitate the six-cube steps, discontinue the steps. If he succeeds either with or without a demonstration, proceed to the ten-cube steps.

The procedure for this is the same as for the six-cube steps, the examiner building behind the screen, letting the child look at the steps, and then knocking down the model and asking the child to make one just like it.

If demonstration is needed, omit the screen. Say, "Watch the way I make it," and with the child watching, build vertically with four cubes in the first column, three in the second, two in the third, and one in the last. As the child looks at the steps, the highest column should be at his right.

*Recording:* As the child works, record the following: The child's verbal responses to directions should be recorded verbatim, as well as a rough description of his activity. Clues given by examiner—use a / mark. When demonstrations are needed, indicate with (*dem.*). Using numbers, reconstruct the sequence and arrangement of the child's product. If the tower tumbled, place a (✔) mark by the number of the last block that stood, that is, the one before the block that tumbled. (Tower on recording sheet is ten cubes high.)

## TABLE 4

### CUBES: NORMATIVE AGE RESPONSES FROM 2½ TO 6 YEARS

SPONTANEOUS:    2½ years—Two-and-a-half-year-olds either build a tower or put the blocks in a row. A large number of children at this age do not indulge in spontaneous block building. They simply hold the blocks or transpose them on the table.

3 years—At 3 years of age, the vertical arrangement is superseded by horizontal alignment. The cubes are arranged horizontally in a row, as a rule.

4 years—The 4-year-old usually builds a complicated structure and names it. Typical structures are towers (usually double) that are called houses, buildings, walls, or chimneys. Frequently several structures are built before the child settles on a single item.

5 years—Five-year-olds often build three-dimensional structures. These are usually called houses. A variety of items are built and named animals or perhaps letters. At this age children build promptly and are then ready for the next task.

6 years—The 6-year-old builds in two dimensions again, usually in the lateral and vertical planes. Naming is the same as at 5 years.

TOWER: 2½ years— Builds tower of eight.
     3 years— Builds tower of ten.
TRAIN: 2½ years—Aligns two or more blocks for train.
     3 years—Adds chimney to own train on first trial. May use the third cube for a second chimney, but, given a second trial, copies model.
BRIDGE: 2½ years—Builds a tower or puts cubes in a row.
     3 years—Imitates bridge after demonstration. May misjudge space between cubes and need to readjust in order to place third cube on top.
    3½–4 years—Can almost invariably build bridge given the model.
GATE: 2½–3 years—Most reject the situation.
     3½ years—Usually rejects the situation, but may attempt the gate.
     4 years—Imitates gate after demonstration.
     4½ years—Builds gate without demonstration, though completed structure may be wobbly.
     5 years—Easily builds the gate presented, from the model, and without demonstration.
STEPS: 4½ years—Cannot build even with demonstration. Will attempt, but his product is a slanted tower without a base that keeps tumbling.
(SIX-CUBE)
     5 years—May need demonstration, but can usually build from model.
    5½–6 years—Builds steps without difficulty.
STEPS: 5½ years—May need demonstration before can succeed.
(TEN-CUBE) 6 years—Usually succeeds without demonstration.

## TABLE 5

### CUBES: REFUSALS OR FAILURES

Very often the manner in which a child carries out or refuses a task yields as much information concerning his developmental level as does the finished product or score. The following patterns describe some of the extraneous behavior observed from age to age in cube building. Even though the test is given here to children 2½ years or older, patterns of younger children are also described so that in situations where a child's performance is below his chronological age, the examiner will have some guidelines.

TOWER: 18 months—Casts cubes.
       Taps cube on table top.
     2 years—Knocks over own tower.
       Removes top cube as examiner places it.
     2½ years—Makes verbal reference to falling.
     3 years—Builds a double tower.
     4 years—Builds a shaky structure.

TRAIN:    18 months—Casts cubes.
       Builds tower.
       Pushes cubes together in a mass.
     2 years—Builds tower on model.
       Hands cube to examiner.
       Brings cube to model but does not release.
       Builds on model.
    2½ years—Reaches for model or pulls toward self.
       Places chimney at each end of train.
BRIDGE:  2 years—Brings cube to model.
   2–2½ years—Builds on model.
   2½–3 years—Builds train.
     3 years—Pushes bridge up to model or may build bridge at an
       angle.
    3½ years—Builds tower
       Builds flat bridge
       Pulls model toward self.
       Fills in doorway of model.
GATE:  2½ years—Builds a tower.
     3 years—Builds a bridge.
       Tries to tilt cube but it falls.
       Pulls model toward self.
   3–3½ years—Knocks down model.
    3½ years—Builds on model.
       Reaches for model.
       Knocks down own when partly built.
     4 years—Uses cube from model.
       Builds side towers but doesn't tilt center cube.
       May build gate at an angle.

## PENCIL AND PAPER TESTS
### (2–6 YEARS)

Next to the cube situations, the pencil and paper tests are perhaps the most basic and significant of all the Gesell Preschool Tests. Copy Forms and Incomplete Man by themselves constitute a very useful screening test in those cases where the full test battery cannot be given.

### THE COPY FORMS TEST

Copy Forms, including imitating Vertical and Horizontal strokes, is a useful and effective test from 2 years of age on through 6 and beyond. Vertical and Horizontal strokes are the outstanding paper and pencil items at 2 and 2½ years of age. However, even by 2½ an examiner can attempt to elicit a circular scribble in response to her own circular stroke, and by 3 and after, imitation or copying of the printed forms (Circle, Cross, Square, Triangle, Divided Rectangle, and Diamond) can be attempted.

Since imitating a form is for most considerably easier than copying, if the child of any age fails at copying the Circle, Cross, or Square, the examiner may make these forms herself and then ask the child to imitate them. More complex forms are merely presented by showing the child the printed card. The examiner does not demonstrate the Triangle, Divided Rectangle, or Diamond.

By 4 and after, the examiner also tries to see if the child can print name or letters and numbers.

All of these Copy Forms tests indicate how simple a test can be and still be revealing. Thus this test consists, obviously, of a series of six forms of increasing difficulty. Its significance lies not only in checking the child's success at copying, but it also shows the way in which the child copies, the size form he makes, and the place on the paper where he chooses to draw his forms. All of these and many more qualifying categories tell as much about the child as do his success or failure in copying the form in question.

The beauty of this test so far as the child is concerned is that if he cannot copy some given form, say the Triangle, chances are that he will be able to copy the earlier form. Thus, from his point of view, he is succeeding, regardless of what our norms may say about his behavior level.

One of the most impressive confirmations of the value of this test comes from Arthur R. Jensen of California who comments that

> Readiness in the cognitive sphere is largely the ability to conceptualize the learning task, to grasp the aim of one's efforts long before achieving mastery of the task. The relative ineffectiveness of shaping one's behavior to external requirements as compared with internal requirements is perhaps seen most dramatically in the child's efforts to copy geometric figures of varying difficulty. Unless the child can internalize conceptual representations of the figure, he cannot copy it even though the model is directly before him.
>
> Partly for this reason, as well as for its correlations with school readiness, the Ilg and Ames figure copying test is probably one of the most convincing and valuable measures of cognitive development in

the preschool years and throughout the primary grades. It shows very clear-cut age differences, and the figures used come close to being a true scale in the Gutman sense. (48)

## HORIZONTAL AND VERTICAL STROKES

*Material:* An 8½-by-11-inch sheet of green paper and a sharp No. 2½ lead pencil. For 2-year-olds, a red lumber crayon may be more acceptable than the usual lead pencil.

*Directions:*  VERTICAL STROKE:

Secure the child's attention and then, using crayon or pencil, draw a straight vertical line near the edge of the paper at the child's left. Say, "Down like this!"

Hand the crayon or pencil to the child and say, "Now you make one like this." If need be, give the child three trials, demonstrating each time on a fresh piece of paper.

HORIZONTAL STROKE:

Use the same procedure except now draw a horizontal line from left to right at the top of the paper as viewed by the child, saying, "Over like this."

Hand the crayon or pencil to the child and say, "Now you make one." Again, if need be, give the child three trials.

## COPY FORMS

*Material:* Copy Form cards: Circle, Cross, Square, Triangle, Divided Rectangle, and the Diamond in two positions.

Sheets of 8½-by-11-inch green paper and sharp No. 2½ lead pencil. Recording sheet.

*Directions:* Place the Copy Form cards in a pile above the upper edge of the child's paper. Indicate the top card which shows a circle and say, "Make one like this on your paper."

DEMONSTRATION OF CIRCLE:

If, as will often be the case at 2 and 2½ years of age, the child refuses to or is unable to copy the circle, examiner demonstrates it. Examiner draws a continuous counterclockwise circle, starting at the top and saying, "Around like this. Now you make it."

This demonstration should come immediately after the child has refused or failed the circle and before going on to the cross. Demonstration of circle (and, if need be, of cross and square) is made at the top of the child's page; but only one demonstration on a page and only one demonstration.

Demonstrations should be fairly large—about two inches in length for each part of cross and each side of square. Terminate the test when a demonstration is failed and the next form is unrecognizable.

DEMONSTRATION OF CROSS:

If child fails the cross, demonstrate by drawing the vertical line first and saying, with emphasis, "Down like this." Then make the horizontal line, going from left to right, and say, "And over like this. *Now you do it.*"

DEMONSTRATION OF SQUARE:

If child fails the square, demonstrate by drawing a square. Make the left-hand vertical line first and then the right-hand vertical line, saying, "Down like this" and "Down like this." Then, make the two horizontal lines, left to right, saying, "Over like this and over like this. *Now you make one.*"

*Further Directions:* Unless demonstration is needed, the examiner indicates the top card on the pile of seven cards. This is the circle. Examiner points to the circle and says, "Make one like this on your paper."

As each form is completed, remove the card so that the next form can be seen and say, "Now make this one." Continue till all forms have been presented.

When the horizontal diamond is shown, the child may ask if he may turn the card. If he does, say, "Try this one this way and then you can do the next one the other way."

*Recording:* Record on recording sheet all comments made by the child as he or she works. Check in the appropriate box the child's dominant hand. Describe pencil grasp. Record direction of strokes with arrows, and also indicate starting points and shifts of paper.

Indicate need for additional questions or encouragement with a / mark.

After the test is completed, transfer to the child's page the directional arrow heads and number of strokes. Draw replicas of any unrecognizable forms above the child's attempt, in small forms.

## TABLE 6
### NORMS FOR COPY FORMS

2½ years: Can imitate horizontal and vertical strokes.
If imitates circle, it is with circular scribble.

3 years: Imitates demonstration of cross with two vertical lines.
Imitates circle with fairly roundish form, started at the top and drawn counter clockwise.
Names square but cannot copy or imitate. All forms more difficult than the cross tend to be mere blobs.

3½ years: Makes a good start but poor finish on circle, but does not need demonstration.

Copies cross, too, without demonstration. Horizontal line may be much longer than vertical line. Some split the horizontal line, making one side with right hand and the other with the left hand.

Needs demonstration for square. In copying may merely make a circle. The square tends to be a rectangle in a vertical or horizontal position.

All forms more difficult than square tend to be mere blobs.

4 years: Circle may be oval shaped. Copies bottom up and clockwise.

Cross may have an elongated vertical line, short horizontal line too far up on vertical line.

Copies square as a circle. With demonstration, makes a reasonably good square.

May attempt triangle, rather unsuccessfully.

4½ years: Circle still oval shaped, copied from the bottom up and drawn clockwise.

Copies cross in elongated vertical position. Copying the square is normative but shape may still be rectangular.

Copy triangle is attempted, with focus on the point. Top tends to be rounded.

Divided rectangle is usually rectangular, but oriented vertically. Center dividing line and many short horizontal lines on each side. Product may resemble an enclosed ladder.

Diamonds are mere blobs.

5 years: Circle better rounded, still starts at bottom and drawn clockwise. Poor closure.

Cross copied quite successfully.

Square, too, copied successfully though one side may be curved, one corner off.

Triangle now has one oblique side but baseline may be off.

Divided rectangle tends to be square, with three short horizontal lines on each side of a center vertical line. Side lines still do not cross center line.

Diamonds may have one side done well, but angles are often exaggerated into knobby points.

Placing all forms on one page is now normative.

5½ years: Lopsided circle. Child may now start at top and draw counterclockwise.

Copies cross.

Copies square; now a rather good square.

Copies triangle with two obliques. Baseline may still be off, but a recognizable triangle is normative.

Divided rectangle: horizontal line may cross center vertical line and about one-third of children also make angled lines which cross center line.

Diamonds may have one good side and other rounded sides.

6 years:   Forms are now copied in a quick gross-motor manner so that closure points may be poor. There is a tendency for lines to overshoot.

Circles are round, start from the top and are drawn counterclockwise.

May make Latin cross with horizontal line too high.

Good square.

Triangles as at 5½.

Divided rectangle: three interior lines now cross center vertical line.

Diamonds are squarish in shape.

## Qualitative Considerations

For several of our test situations, a careful qualitative observation and recording of the way the child responds can be quite as informative as the actual scoring. Two of the situations in which such qualitative considerations are especially important are Copy Forms and the Incomplete Man.

In Copy Form situations described above, each form provides special things which may be noted by the experienced examiner. Perhaps the two most telling are Copy Circle and Divided Rectangle. For Copy Circle the two important qualitative observations are the place of starting and the direction of drawing.

The most common age sequence that can be observed if one follows an individual child longitudinally is that the very youngest child to make a circle tends to start at the top and to draw counterclockwise. His circle is usually big and wobbly and the ends may not meet.

As the child grows older, his circle starts at the bottom and is drawn clockwise. Then, with considerably increased maturity, the circle again starts at the top and is drawn counterclockwise.*

Though we find substantial individual differences, in general, the early starting at the top and drawing counterclockwise occurs at 3 and possibly at 3½. From 3½ to 4 years of age on through 5, most start at the bottom and draw clockwise. Only at 5 in girls and 6 years of age in boys do most once again manage to start at the top and to draw counterclockwise. Girls tend to be about six months ahead of boys in this respect. After 6 years of age, the bottom-up clockwise circle is considered by us to be a sign of immaturity.

The second Copy Form in which qualitative aspects are of special

* These trends tend to be noted in left-handed as well as right-handed boys and girls. However, if a left-handed child continues to draw the circle bottom up and clockwise after 6 years of age, this handedness factor must be kept in mind and in his/her case this type of circle should not necessarily be considered an immaturity.

importance is the Divided Rectangle. Individual differences in the reproduction of this form are very great, so that percentages for any one type of drawing are seldom high. But roughly this is what we may expect:

At the earliest ages the outside of the form may be roughly circular in shape. Gradually, around 4½ years of age, in many it assumes a squarish form. At 5, the outside varies: it may be a square, a vertical rectangle, or correctly a horizontal rectangle. At 5½, the horizontal rectangle, though not yet normative, predominates in girls. Boys still make square or rectangular forms in about equal numbers. By 6, both can be expected to make a correct horizontal rectangle.

The inside markings vary even more individually. At 4 years of age, they may be no more than a network of scribbles. At 4½, they may likely consist of a vertical stroke bisecting the form, with three or more short straight lines on either side of the vertical stroke.

By 5, the short side lines tend to slant, but still do not cross the center line. It is only by 5½ that a substantial number, approximately one-third, make a horizontal line and two angled lines which cross the center line. A horizontal line and two angled lines all of which cross the center are not normative in either sex till 6 years of age; and all four lines do not cross at some single central point till long after that.

### Organization on Page

Quite as telling as the way the individual forms are copied is the organization of all forms on the page. Rather clear age changes are evident in this respect, the range being from the very large one-form-to-a-page of the young preschooler to the single horizontal row or several horizontal rows taking up half a page or even less at later ages.

### Space Used

Children under 4 tend to require one whole page for each form imitated or copied. Even at 4 and 4½, the majority use more than one page for all forms. Improvement sets in at 5 years, when 72% of girls, 68% of boys, need only one-half to one page for all forms. From 5½ years, substantial numbers of both sexes require even less than half a page. Table 7 presents these data in tabular form.

## Place on Paper

The overall age trend is for figures to become smaller and for less and less of the page to be used with increasing age. As Table 7 shows, even 5-year-olds tend to use the whole page, more or less. From 5½, the largest number of subjects place forms in horizontal rows, though this does not become normative in girls until 7 years, in boys until 10.

TABLE 7

COPY FORMS: ORGANIZATION ON PAGE

| | 3½ Years* | | 4 Years* | | 4½ Years* | | 5 Years | | 5½ Years | | 6 Years | | 7 Years | |
|---|---|---|---|---|---|---|---|---|---|---|---|---|---|---|
| | G | B | G | B | G | B | G | B | G | B | G | B | G | B |
| **Amount of Space Used** | | | | | | | | | | | | | | |
| More than 1 page | 87 | 95 | 65 | 72 | 52 | 68 | 6 | 10 | 8 | 4 | 4 | 2 | 2 | 4 |
| ½ to 1 page | 13 | 5 | 32 | 25 | 38 | 27 | 72 | 68 | 50 | 56 | 60 | 50 | 60 | 40 |
| Less than ½ page | 0 | 0 | 3 | 3 | 10 | 5 | 22 | 22 | 42 | 40 | 36 | 48 | 38 | 56 |
| **Arrangement on Paper** | | | | | | | | | | | | | | |
| Random | | | | | | | 52 | 32 | 26 | 32 | 26 | 30 | 22 | 18 | 16 | 18 |
| Circular | | | | | | | 20 | 46 | 42 | 42 | 28 | 16 | 26 | 16 | 18 | 16 |
| Vertical | | | | | | | 10 | 10 | 2 | 12 | 8 | 6 | 10 | 14 | 10 | 14 |
| Horizontal | | | | | | | 14 | 12 | 28 | 12 | 32 | 38 | 36 | 44 | 52 | 48 |
| H & V mixed | | | | | | | 4 | 0 | 2 | 2 | 6 | 10 | 6 | 8 | 4 | 4 |
| **Relative Size of Individual Forms** | | | | | | | | | | | | | | |
| Variable | | | | | | | 70 | 56 | 42 | 54 | 40 | 46 | 38 | 30 | 24 | 34 |
| Getting larger | | | | | | | 8 | 16 | 6 | 14 | 14 | 24 | 20 | 30 | 22 | 18 |
| Getting smaller | | | | | | | 20 | 28 | 24 | 20 | 20 | 8 | 12 | 22 | 6 | 20 |
| Even | | | | | | | 2 | 0 | 28 | 12 | 26 | 22 | 30 | 18 | 48 | 28 |

*The data for 3½, 4, and 4½-year-olds are from preschool data, the rest from *School Readiness*.

From 5 through 7 years, substantial numbers of children place forms in more or less shapeless bunches. An increasing number arrange figures in neatly boxed squares in one of the four quadrants of the page, though percentages for this are always small.

There are some children who need to make multiple starts. This is more common at 5 years. And there is the child who shifts his paper repeatedly so that he may execute each stroke as a vertical stroke toward himself or away from himself. This suggests difficulty in orienting to a given position. The only way such a child can solve his problem is to shift the environment, in this case the paper.

## Arrangement of Forms on Page

Through 4½ years of age, arrangement of forms on a page tends to be random or at the very best somewhat circular. At 5, more pattern is coming in. Many now place a rather large circle somewhere near the center of the page and arrange other forms around it more or less in order and in a somewhat circular orientation.

By 5½, forms may be balanced by placing the cross on one side of the circle and the square on its other side. Other forms are usually scattered on the page. Or there may be no clear order for any of the forms.

At 6 years, the first four forms tend to be organized. They may be either paired with circle and cross on one line and triangle and divided rectangle under them. Or all four forms may be placed horizontally on one line, with others in varying positions.

## Relative Size of Individual Forms

Through 4½ years of age in girls, 5 years in boys, the several forms are highly variable in size. Not until 7 years do most of the girls, though only 28% of the boys, achieve a more or less evenness of size.

FIGURE 2 Organization on Page

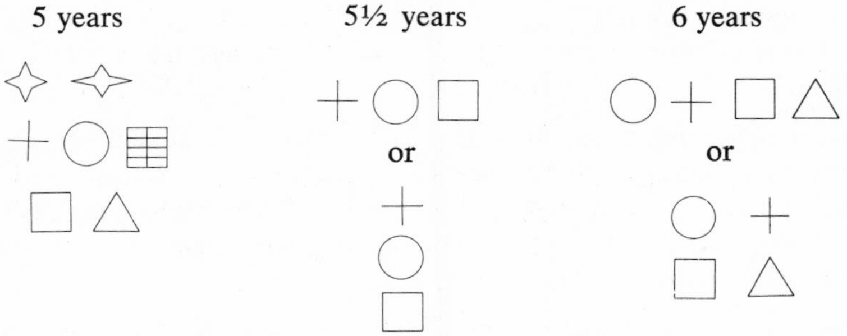

5 years  5½ years  6 years

## THE INCOMPLETE MAN TEST

The Incomplete Man Test was introduced by Dr. Gesell in 1925. The figure with its missing parts provides a stimulating challenge and is often a favorite part of the examination. Except for the eyes, each of the missing parts has a model already drawn to guide the child.

The type, angle, length, and shape of each part, especially the arm and the tie, allow for many stages of perception and therefore of execution. The addition of parts is a main focus in evaluation of the child's response. However, the way he names the figure and the quality of his performance are also significant, as will be explained.

The 2½- and 3-year-old resist any prolonged involvement, and so the examiner needs to present the task quickly, expecting only brief interest. The 3½-year-old will be able to sustain interest longer and will complete specific parts with recognizable strokes. From 4 years through 10 years, this test is well accepted by most children, and the response can be extremely revealing to the examiner.

*Material:* Examiner—Recording sheet. Child—Incomplete Man form and a sharp No. 2½ lead pencil.

*Procedure:* Place the blue sheet of paper on which is printed the Incomplete Man form in front of the child on the table. Ask, "What does this look like to you?"

If the child responds, say, "You finish him." If he does not respond, say, "You finish him and *then* you can tell me."

After the man has been completed, the examiner asks the following questions:

"How does he look?"

"How does he feel inside?" (If the child responds either "Happy" or "Sad," skip the next question.)

"Is he happy or sad?"

"How can you tell?"

If the child has trouble with any of these questions, do not pursue them.

*General Directions:* If the child lags in his completion of salient parts, he may be encouraged with either a suggested or a direct clue. The suggested clue: "Is there anything else missing?" The direct clue: "Is there anything else missing here?" while pointing with a pencil to the general area of the missing part.

*Recording:* Record the child's responses verbatim at the bottom of page in the space under the heading "Incomplete Man."

Completions which follow suggested clues, that is, examiner has asked, "Is there anything else missing?" are recorded by a broken line preceding the name of the part, thus———*hair.*

Completions which follow direct clues, that is, the examiner has pointed to the general area of the missing part and asked, "Is there anything else missing here?" are recorded by a solid line preceding the name of the part, thus———ear.

As the child adds parts, list them vertically at the bottom of the examiner's recording sheet on the left side. Responses to the inquiry questions are recorded in the space at the lower right-hand side of the page, under the heading: "When completed, ask. . . ."

Abbreviations which may be used:

bl = body line
nl = neckline
ll = looks like
idk = I don't know
hl = How does he look?
fi = How does he feel inside?
hs = Is he happy or sad?
ht = How can you tell?

(Plus any other abbreviations which the individual examiner wishes to use.)

*Summary Recording:* When testing has been completed, transfer the child's responses to the inquiry questions to the child's paper.

### Arm

The Incomplete Man Test, with its many parts to be added, provides one of the best opportunities for making comparisons between responses given at successive ages by any individual child.

The added part which to us is perhaps the most revealing is the arm. Though our norms do not entirely bear out this observation (that is, we cannot guarantee that all children will follow this path), superior children, if followed individually, tend to respond as follows:

An arm, when first added, tends to be added low on the body line. With increased age it moves upward till eventually it slants upward, matching the arm provided. At the earliest ages the added arm tends to be excessively long, but at the same time that it is moving upward, it gradually becomes shorter and shorter until it matches the arm provided in length. A third change which takes place with age is that, though when first added the arm points downward, as the child grows older the arm is drawn at right angles to the body line (about at waist level) and finally points upward as does the arm provided.

That is, with increased age, the arm that is added moves upward on the body line, gradually shortens in length, and shifts direction from downward to upward. Around 4 years in many, the arm starts at about waist level and points straight out. There is also a tendency in some for the added arm to cross the body line, though in girls by 4½ and in boys by 5 years it is expected to meet the body line neatly and not cross over.

Girls as a rule make an arm of more or less correct length by 6 years, boys not till later. The arm points up for girls by 5½–6, for boys at 5 years and following.

### Leg

Though both girls and boys add some leg by 3 years of age, and some kind of foot by 3½, and point the foot correctly toward the right by 4½ years of age, there is great variability in the kind of leg and foot made, and in their placement, from child to child and from age to age.

*The leg, more than any other part added, often becomes less accurate as the child grows older.* It seems in many that the greater effort which accompanies added awareness, at the older ages, results in diminished accuracy.

In general, younger children add a leg which is much too long. The leg added by girls is likely to be of more or less a good length by 5 years of age; by boys by 5½. The foot tends to be too long in both boys and girls through 6 years of age, though a too long foot is normative in girls only at 4½ years, in boys only at 4½ and 5½ years.

Though many children by 5 years of age manage a reasonably good placement of the leg on the body line, fully accurate placement is not achieved during the first six years.

In general, with added age, the trend for leg and foot is for both gradually to become shorter, for the foot to turn from leftward to rightward, and for placement to improve, though marked inaccuracy persists well past the preschool ages. An inaccurate leg and foot are not unusual long after other parts have become reasonably accurate.

### Neck

Treatment of the neck area is extremely variable from child to child, though it is most revealing of maturity level especially from 4 through 7 years. In perhaps the majority, expected responses are as follows:

Body line at neck area is extended to meet knot of tie by 3½ years in girls, by 4 years in boys. A next stage (though this never becomes normative) is that the child makes a curved line extending from face line to end of body line as given.

A straight neck as well as extension of body line is added at 5½ by girls, at 6 by boys. The bow is usually, though not always, the last of the three parts to be drawn.

Body line, neck, and bow *(all three)* are not normative even by 6 years of age, though by 6 many are struggling with the bow. Body line, neck, and bow are *each* normative in both sexes by 6 years of age, but not necessarily all three in the same child and not accurately drawn.

### Eyes

Individual differences are very great, but there is a tendency for eyes when first added to be roundish scribbles. Gradually they become either small filled-in dots or open circles. It is not till well past the preschool years that eyes take on an oval shape and/or are given pupils.

However, placement of eyes shows considerable improvement with age even in the preschool years. Eyes in girls tend to match in their vertical placement as early as 4 years of age, in boys by 4½ years. They match in size in girls by 5, in boys by 5½. Horizontal placement does not match in most till 6 years or later.

### Hair

Some hairs are added by girls by 3½ years, by boys by 4 years. The correct number of hairs, correctly graduated, is not achieved during the first 6 years of life, but hair of a reasonably good length may be managed by girls at 4½ years of age, by boys at 5.

Though in most respects, with hair as with other body parts, girls achieve a correct or at least an adequate performance sooner than do boys, good hair placement is normative in boys but not in girls by 6 years of age. Girls more than boys have a tendency from 4½ through 6 years to continue hair down too far toward the neck area.

### Ear

Some effort at adding an ear is made by girls as early as 3½ years, by boys at 4½ years and following. Ear form and size are both extremely variable. Very young children tend to make the ear too big. With added age, it comes closer to the ear provided on the printed form, but placement and shape remain highly variable.

## Extra Parts

Extra parts are added by some children right through 6 years of age, but the adding of extra parts is normative in girls only through 4½ years, in boys through 5 years.

The extra part most added is a belly button. In girls this is seen most at 4 and 4½ years; in boys at 3, 3½, and 5 years. There is a tendency for some children at 5 to start what might have been a belly button and then to cover this inclination by adding more dots or circles and saying, "That's buttons on his coat."

A very small number of children in the age range from 3 to 5 years add breasts or genitals. This seems to occur most often at 3 years of age, but even then it is rare. Scribbling over the figure or over part of the figure is seen most often at 2½ and 3 years of age in both boys and girls, and at 3½ in boys.

Marks are made on the figure's nose or mouth by a few children at all ages. An extra arm or leg or fingers are seen to some extent, but they are not normative at any age.

Some children at 3½ and 4 draw over the lines already there, or they will reproduce the figure at one side of the paper. Encircling the whole or part of the figure is conspicuous in girls at 3 and in boys at 3 and 3½ years of age.

### TABLE 8
### INCOMPLETE MAN TEST: AGE NORMS FROM 2½ TO 6 YEARS
### (COMPLETION OF PARTS)

2½ years: May add an arm or leg or may merely scribble over figure.

3 years: Most add three parts: arm, leg, and possibly eyes. May make marks outside the figure.

> *Eyes:* Large open circles or open scribbles by girls. Boys make eyes of varied types and sizes.
> *Leg:* Normative in both sexes, but usually much too long. Foot may be added. If so, may point to the left. Leg and foot may be a single stroke.
> *Arm:* Added by more than half. Placed too low, too long, direction variable.

3½ years: Most add three or four parts: arm, leg, eyes, and possibly one other. Children no longer scribble on the form but may encircle head, body, or total figure. May also make marks outside the figure.

> *Eyes:* Large open circles, uneven in size.

*Leg:* Long and with some type of foot added.

*Arm:* Points down and is long. Some attempt at fingers.

*Hair:* Girls may attempt but do not make individual hairs; mostly scribbles. Boys as a rule do not attempt.

*Neck Area:* Girls may or may not extend body line to meet given tie.

*Ear:* Both sexes may attempt.

4 years: There is marked sex difference here: girls on the average add five-and-a-half parts; boys, on the average, only three.

*Eyes:* Large unmatched circles which, in girls, match in vertical placement.

*Leg:* Leg and foot made in separate strokes, both too long.

*Arm:* Long, and fingers added.

*Hair:* From four to seven hairs made by both sexes. In girls, hair is too short; in boys, too long. Placed low by boys, but rather well placed by many girls.

*Neck Area:* Boys as well as girls extend given body line to meet knot in tie.

*Ear:* More girls than boys make ear.

4½ years: Girls on the average now add seven parts, boys five. It is at this age that many complete the figure in a "wild" manner.

*Eyes:* Large open circles which in both sexes match in vertical placement.

*Leg:* Leg and foot are made in a single stroke by girls. Boys use two strokes. Both sexes have foot pointing to the right. Both make a too long leg.

*Arm:* Now meets body line when made by girls. Boys tend to extend their line into the body. Girls more than boys make a too long arm. Arm is now drawn straight out from the body, or may slant upward.

*Hair:* In some, hair circles the entire head.

*Neck Area:* Body line only is made. Line stops at knot in tie.

*Ear:* Both sexes now make an ear.

5 years: Now add eight parts.

*Eyes:* Boys make large open circles; girls make open circles or filled-in dots. Eyes may match in size.

*Leg:* Both sexes make leg and foot in single stroke, usually good length.

*Arm:* Both sexes have an arm which meets body line and does not cross it.

*Hair:* Good length but placed low.

*Neck Area:* Body line only, meets knot. Or some now make a slanted combination of neck and body line.

*Ear:* Both sexes add ear.

5½ years: Performance of the two sexes comes a bit closer. Girls on the average add eight parts, boys, seven.

*Eyes:* Open circles, getting smaller. Eyes made by girls match in vertical placement but not in horizontal. Eyes made by boys match in size and vertical placement.

*Leg:* Made in one stroke. Now becoming shorter. Usually good length.

*Arm:* Beginning to move upward and to point upward.

*Hair:* Good length. Girls place hair too low while boys have good placement. Both sexes make from four to seven hairs.

*Neck Area:* Body line, neck, and bow now seen with many girls, though addition of all three parts is not normative. Boys nearly reach normative level in making body line and neck. Neck line generally consists of a two-part straight neck and body line.

*Ear:* Now 95% of girls, 82% of boys add an ear. Placement is highly variable; size is either good or too small. Beginning effort at correct shaping of ear, not too successful.

6 years: The average child now adds nine parts: arm and hand, leg and foot, hair, ear, eyes, and at least two parts at the neck line.

*Eyes:* Girls make an open circle or dot. Eyes do not match in size or placement. Varied types are seen with boys: large circle, blacked in, or dot. Eyes match in size and vertical placement and may match in horizontal placement.

*Leg:* Good length. Foot now turned to the right.

*Arm:* Good length with girls. Both sexes have arm pointing upward.

*Hair:* Four to seven hairs in boys. Girls may make correct number (eight to ten). Length of hair is good, but placement is low. Boys have good length, good placement.

*Neck Area:* Many now are struggling with the tie. Body line, neck, and bow are all normative, though not all three in any one child.

*Ear:* All now add an ear, but correct placement is still not normative. Size is variable. Only 35% attempt correct shape.

## *Naming Incomplete Man and Responses to Projection Questions*

Naming the Incomplete Man becomes normative at 3 years of age in both boys and girls. However, it is not until 5 years that any one special response becomes normative. At that time "Man" is given by boys.

The most typical preschool names include "Boy," "Little boy," "Person," "Girl," "Lady," "Snowman," "Scarecrow."

At 5 years of age, "Boy" and "Man" are the most usual responses and these remain consistent favorites through 6 years and following. "Part" or "Half of a man" begins at 4½ years of age and continues through 6, but here again is not normative.

During the years from 4 to 6, responses to the Projection Questions of "How does he look?" "How does he feel inside?" "Is he happy or sad?" and "How can you tell?" show the following patterns:

*How does he look?*
    4 years—Typical response is funny, fine, all right, OK.
    5 years—Very positive. Many say "good."
    6 years—May express some negative emotion: sad, unhappy. A more literal child may say, "He looks like a man."

*How does he feel inside?*
  4 years—Awful, sick, bad.
  5 years—May persist in his "good," but often says "happy" or "sad."
    The very literal child may say "soft," "hard." Some feel the
    paper and say, "He feels like paper!"

*Happy or Sad?*
  Even when initial response to "looks like" and "feels inside" may
    have been positive, this question often stimulates the re-
    sponse of "sad."
  5½ years—Now may say "mad." Or may mention both kinds of emo-
    tion: "He's happy and he's sad" or "He looks good, but
    feels sad."

*How can you tell?*
  4 years—"Cause"; "I know"; "Because I gave him everything he
    needs."
  5 years—"Happy" predominates. Some refer to the mouth.
  5½ years—"He's happy cause he's got a smile."
  6 years—More negative emotions coming in now. Some refer to
    man's "frown."

## Qualitative Considerations

For the first 30 years or so of the life of this unique test, scoring
was solely in terms of how many parts the child added to the man.
For the beginning examiner this counting of parts remains the simplest, surest, and most effective measure.

The experienced examiner also may score this test primarily for
number of parts added, but her total evaluation may be quite as
much in terms of the way the man looks as in the sheer number of
parts.

In the years from 2½ to 5, the part which may tell the most is the
arm. As noted just earlier, with added age the arm tends to change
in three major ways. When first added, it begins low on the body
line, points downward, and is far too long. As the child grows older,
the arm moves upward till it finally matches in place of origin the
printed arm. It also becomes gradually shorter. And with time it
shifts from pointing downward to pointing straight out to pointing
upward to match, again, the printed form.

Also, arm as well as leg, when first added, slashes right across the
given body line. It is only with increasing age that the child is able
to start these two additions right at the body line, without crossing.

From 4 through 7, some of the best qualitative clues are found in the child's treatment of the neck area. The first part added in this area, usually around 4 years of age, is an extension of the body line, closing the pictured gap. Next, often around 5, a curving line closes the gap from face line to end of body line as given. Next, around 5½, a straight neck plus an extension of the body line are made. And some boys and girls begin to try to add a bow. The bow is added increasingly often, so that by 6 years of age body line, neck, and bow are each normative. But all three do not necessarily appear together. By 6½, most do make all three parts, but not smoothly. In the majority it will be 7 years of age before the neck area is completed smoothly and effectively with all three added parts. Or by then the bow may be so nicely rounded that it takes merely two additions—short, straight neck and bow—to complete the area effectively.

Next in time sequence comes the treatment of the eyes. These reveal their significant story right along, but become increasingly telling in the older ages. First of all comes the matter of matching in horizontal and vertical placement and in size and type. Eyes match in vertical placement as early as 4 or 4½ years of age; in size, around 5 or 5½; in horizontal placement, not till 6 years or later. The oval shape which most resembles the human eye, as well as pupils, are not achieved in the first 6 years of life.

Age changes in other parts are indicated in the text, just earlier. For instance, the leg, like the arm, is at first much too long. It gradually becomes shorter and better placed, and the foot turns from pointing toward the left to pointing toward the right. Hairs, too, at first are too long; they gradually become shorter and of graduated length, like the model.

But in general it may be the arm, neck area, and eyes which give the most clear-cut qualitative clues to the age level of the child's response.


## LETTERS, NAME, AND NUMBERS* (4–6 YEARS)

*Material:* Sheet of green paper 8½-by-11-inches and a sharp No. 2½ lead pencil. For examiner, recording sheet.

---

* At 4 years and following, this writing of letters, name, and numbers may precede the Copy Forms situations, coming just before the Copy Circle.

*Procedure:* For children 4 years and older, ask, "Can you write your name?" If the child cannot, ask, "Can you write any letters, like the letter 'A' or the first letter of your own name?"

Do not push this if the child is reluctant to or unable to conform.

If the child is able to write (usually print) his name, he will usually do so. If he cannot print his name but can print letters, he usually starts right out with letters.

However, if he does print his first name, the examiner will then pursue the situation by asking if he can print his last name or just the first letter of his last name.

If the child is able to print merely letters, the examiner then asks, "Can you write any numbers?" If there is no response, ask, "Can you write a number 1?"

These questions are asked of children of an appropriate age before the examiner presents the Copy Form cards. There is no recording sheet provided. The child's own product constitutes the record.

### TABLE 9
### NORMS FOR WRITING NAME AND LETTERS

| | |
|---|---|
| 4½ years: | Prints one or two recognizable letters. |
| 5 years: | Prints first name. |
| 5½ years: | Prints first name and first letter of last name. |
| 6 years: | Prints first and last names (girls). |
| 6½ years: | Prints first and last names (boys). |

### TABLE 10
### NORMS FOR WRITING NUMBERS

| | |
|---|---|
| 2½, 3, 3½ years: | Most children of these ages do not make numbers. A few 3½-year-olds will use markings in an attempt to do so. |
| 4 years: | Understanding of the written symbols is just beginning. Some attempt at random numbers is made by a few at this age. Numbers made are large, and only a few are attempted. |
| 4½ years: | The numbers from 1 to 4 are tried by many, and many can make one or two recognizable numbers. Numbers are large and may be reversed in position. They are placed at random on the page. |
| 5 years: | Some can make numbers up to 5. However, many confuse letters and numbers. Others make a series of vertical strokes to represent numbers. If they can write in sequence, may omit some. Some are beginning to place their numbers in a horizontal line, though many con- |

tinue to place at random. Numbers are large (½ to 2 inches).

5½ years: Many now can write numbers from 1 to 11 or even higher. Most organize in a horizontal line. A sizable number at this age reverse numbers. Size of numbers still rather large (½ to 1 inch).

6 years: Now the ability to write to 20 is close to a normative level. Numbers are organized in a horizontal position. If a second line is needed, it usually is placed from left to right under the first line. However, if space is not available, numbers will be placed wherever there is room, along the edge of the page or around existing copy forms.

The size of numbers varies at this age. There is a tendency for them to get larger as the task becomes more difficult, or smaller as available space diminishes.

Double numbers may be reversed, with 20 usually written as 02. Also teen numbers still present difficulties and 12 may become 21, etc. This confusion with teen numbers is most often seen during the 5½- to 6-year-old reversal stage. The number of reversed combined digits or of writing single numbers backward is noticeably reduced by 6 years of age.

Baseline is uneven. Spacing may be good with numbers from 1 to 10 but becomes less good with the teens.

## THREE-HOLE FORMBOARD

The Three-Hole Formboard, as well as the Color Forms test which is described next but may be given at any point in the examination which seems suitable, are tests which most 2- and 3-year-old children enjoy. In general, 4-year-olds have gone beyond these tasks which are too easy for most.

Both items are often a welcome relief for the 2- to 3-year-old who may have become fatigued by both verbal and paper-and-pencil tasks. The child's lack of interest in prolonged sedentary or merely verbal occupations, short attention span, and strong locomotor drive create a need for variety of materials and activities. The gamelike quality of these two puzzles catches and holds the young child's interest.

In the overall scheme of the test, these activities offer flexibility and can be brought in at any point when the examiner feels that she may be losing the child. They are especially helpful when there is a need to introduce a simple task to break up a series of relatively difficult situations.

*Material:* Examiner—Recording sheet. Child—Formboard: half-inch board 36 by 16 cm. in size, dark green in color. Three holes are cut equidistant from each other and from the edges of the board from left to right as follows: circle, diameter 8.7 cm.; equilateral triangle, 9.3 cm.; square, 7.5 cm. Three white wooden forms to fit the holes, each 2 cm. thick: circle, diameter 8.5 cm.; equilateral triangle, 9 cm.; square, 7.3 cm.

*General Directions:* The child's attention must be secured for both demonstration of insertion and the rotation of the board. Allow the child to sit or stand as he prefers. When the board is rotated, it should be turned slowly so that the child can see its motion, but not so slowly that his attention wanders.

This test situation is one in which the child's performance can be affected favorably or adversely by the procedure. Urging at the proper moments, showing approval when a successful insertion is made, and being generally encouraging and responsive help the child to do his best.

Most 2½- to 3-year-old children are immediately attracted by the board and blocks. They work long and persistently at the task of insertion. It is the unusual child who does not quickly become involved. Even these children usually apply themselves well when it is re-presented later in the examination, assuming they have failed to respond to the initial presentation.

The formboard offers an excellent means of testing the child's form discrimination ability, attention span, and general adaptability. The behavior required, putting the blocks into their corresponding holes, is such a spontaneous activity that verbal directions may be kept to a minimum.

*Procedure:* Place the formboard on the table so that the round hole is at the child's right, the apex of the triangle directed away from him. Then place the three blocks in front of their respective holes at the edge near the child.

When the child places all the blocks in their holes, lift the board and rotate it 180°, keeping its plane horizontal to the table, and replace it on the table with the square hole near the round block and the round hole near the square block. When the child has completed the first trial, reorient the board by lifting and turning as before. Give the child three trials.

Initially as the board is placed before the child, say, "Put the blocks where they belong."

If the child merely piles the blocks or otherwise does not conform to the expected response, point to the holes, saying, "Put them here."

If he does not fully insert the block, say, "Way in." If necessary, give the block a push, completing or demonstrating full insertion.

*Recording:* As the child works, record rotation successes with a check mark ( ✔ ) and failures with a minus sign ( − ).

TABLE 11 AGE NORMS FOR THREE-HOLE FORMBOARD RESPONSES

2 years:    Places blocks on board spontaneously and inserts with help; adapts to rotation in four trials.

2½ years:   Inserts three blocks on presentation; adapts to rotation with repeated error.

3 years:    Adapts immediately to rotation, with no error or immediate correction of error.

## COLOR FORMS (2–3 YEARS)

This test, like the Three-Hole Formboard, is one which has a fairly short life span, but which is extremely useful and well accepted during the years when it is pertinent.

Many 2-year-olds will accept the situation but do not respond meaningfully. By 2½, the average boy or girl can place one form correctly. By 3 years, the norm is three correct placements, and many children of course do better than this. This test is usually not given after 3½ or 4 years of age.

This test, which is slightly more difficult than the Three-Hole Formboard, nicely bridges the gap between ages when the child fits a form, or forms, into the formboard and the time when he is able to identify and copy the geometric forms (if given).

*Material:* Examiner—Recording sheet showing five cut-out geometric color forms. Child—Five red forms pasted on a white card 8½ by 11 inches. Circle: 5 cm. in diameter (upper right); square: 5 cm. (upper left); triangle: 6.5 cm. (lower left); semicircle: 8 cm. in diameter (lower right); Maltese cross: 7 cm. in length and 2.5 cm. in width of arms (center). Five red cardboard shapes of corresponding size and shape.

*Procedure:* Place the card of color forms on the table before the child so that the semicircle is in the lower right-hand corner as he faces it.

Say, "Oh, look," pointing to each form on the card. Then place the cut-out circle on the card of color forms above the cross. Say, "Where is the other one? Show me the other one just like this." Or ask, "Where does this one go?"

If the child does not respond correctly, point first to the circle and then to the cut-out circle, saying, "See, they are just alike." Bring the cut-out circle close to the circle on the card.

Present the other cut-out forms (triangle, semicircle, square, and cross). Do not indicate, as with the circle, the correct form until all forms have been presented and the child has been asked, for each, "Where does this one go?"

*Recording:* Record with a check mark (✔) if the child succeeds. Use a minus sign (−) if the child does not succeed.

## TABLE 12
### AGE NORMS FOR COLOR FORMS

2 years:   Does not identify any forms.

2½ years:  Places at least one form correctly. The circle, semicircle, or cross appear to be easier to identify and place than do the square or triangle.

3 years:   Places at least three of the forms correctly.

### COUNTING

*Material:* Examiner—Recording sheet.

*Procedure:* Say, "How high can you count?" Regardless of child's response, examiner then says, "Count as far as you can, or until I tell you to stop."

If the child begins to count spontaneously rather than answering your question, permit this.

Stop the spontaneous counting at 40.

### COUNTING PENNIES

If the child counts correctly to 20, skip counting pennies and present the calculation problems. If the child cannot count to 10 or more, skip the calculation problems entirely and present counting pennies.

*Procedure:* Place 4 pennies 2 inches apart in a row on the table. Say, "Count these pennies and tell me how many there are."

If the child hesitates, say, "See like this: 1 . . ."

If the child counts without pointing, demonstrate. Say, "No, count them with your finger like this: 1 . . ."

When the child finishes counting, say, "How many are there altogether?"

If the child correctly counts 4, and gives the correct total, then place 10 pennies in a row and repeat the procedure.

If he succeeds with 10, try 13, and then 20. (Place the 13 and 20 in two rows.)

Give the child two trials if needed.

*Recording:* If the child is asked to count the pennies, use a check mark (✔) to indicate that he counted correctly. Or record the response given verbatim if it is incorrect. Also record the child's response to "How many altogether?"

## CALCULATION

*Procedure:* Say, "If you have _____ pennies and I give you _____ more, how many would you have?" Or (for subtraction), say, "If you have _____ pennies and I take away _____, how many would you have?"

Continue presenting problems until the child indicates by his incorrect responses that he cannot go on.

Present the problems in the following order:

(a) 2 + 2 =     (d) 7 + 3 =     (f) 14 + 3 =
(b) 2 + 3 =     (e) 6 − 4 =     (g) 16 − 4 =
(c) 5 − 2 =

Ask, after each problem is answered, "How did you get it?" If the child gives an incorrect answer, say, "Think again."

If he continues to respond incorrectly, use pennies to help him solve the problem. Allow the child to use his fingers if he starts to do so.

*Recording:* Record verbatim the child's response on page under *Calculation.*

## TABLE 13
### COUNTING AND CALCULATION

| | |
|---|---|
| 3 years: | Counts, with correct pointing, 3 objects. |
| 4 years: | Counts 4 objects |
| 4½ years: | Counts 4 objects and tells "How many?" |
| 5 years: | Counts 10 objects correctly. |
| 5½ years: | Counts 12 objects correctly. |
| 6 years: | Counts 13+ objects correctly. |
| 6½ years: | Adds and subtracts within 10. |

# 6

# Language Behavior

The use of language is a highly individual matter. Some preschoolers, especially girls, may be jabbering away as early as 15 months of age. By 2 years, they may be speaking quite intelligibly in short sentences. Some late-talking boys, equally intelligent, may be pointing more than speaking as late as 2 years of age and may not be saying too much even at 2½.

Some children around 15 to 21 months go through an extremely fluent jargon stage. They seem to want so much to communicate that they do so in their own way even before they have many "real" words.

The variations in language behavior among even perfectly normal children make lists of how many words on the average may be expected at different ages perhaps more anxiety-provoking than useful. And yet even the not-too-verbal tend to go through more or less the same sequences in the development of language as do the highly verbal.

Thus, in spite of rather marked individual differences, it seems fair to present norms for language as for other behaviors.

Every age has its own special language characteristics, as described earlier in Chapter 3. So at 18 months, though jargon may be fluent in some, gesture for many is perhaps the chief means of communication. The most one can expect in the majority of children is a two-word sentence.

At 2, or at the latest at 2½, language blossoms. Language is not only useful but it is also fun. Most can not only make their wants and needs known verbally, they can also share thoughts and some ideas. Vocabulary has grown by leaps and bounds and sentences have increased in length from three words to many more. Language is used socially with contemporaries as well as with adults.

The 3- and the 3½-year-old characteristically have a good command of language and also love words for their own sake. Children of these ages not only use language fluently, but certain words, by their very characteristics, motivate them. They respond especially well if told that something is "new," "different," "exciting," "a surprise."

FOUR, in language as in other ways, is characteristically out-of-bounds. As mentioned earlier, he boasts, he brags, he lies, he even resorts to profanity. Language is now his tool, and he uses it effectively in his efforts to control his world. He also uses it socially, eagerly sharing with others his love of the silly and absurd. Nonsense rhymes and nonsense language both delight him.

FIVE, now a master of ordinary language usage, employs his language to express his delightfully good adjustment. He compliments. He concurs. He tells the world what a good boy he plans to be, how at peace he is with himself and with the universe. Since that time, so few years before, when he uttered his first word, he has come light years in his effective use of language.

For a more detailed summary of characteristic age changes in language behavior, the reader is referred to Chapter 3. What follows are instructions for giving, as well as our findings about, the various tests which make up the language section of our Gesell Preschool Test Battery.

## REPORTED EARLY LANGUAGE (12–30 MONTHS)

As with items under personal-social behavior, this information will have to be obtained from the parent, although the examiner will of course record any words or phrases heard during the examination.

*(a.) Vocabulary (12–24 months):* Ask the parent how many words the child uses and what they are. Ask especially whether he or she says, "Mama," "Dada," "No," "Bye-bye," "Doggie," "Go," "Out," and other common words. Also ask if the child has names for people, toys, pets, food, clothes, etc.

*(b.) Jargon (12–24 months):* If this is not heard during the examination, ask about it. Find out if the child uses jargon, if it sounds like real conversation. Does the child seem to think he is saying

something? Does his jargon consist mostly of repetitions of a few sounds or is it varied in character?

*(c.) Extent to which child combines words (15–24 months):* Ask, "Does he put words together of his own accord?" Get as many examples as you can. Ask especially for the longest combination that the parent has heard. Ask if child says things like, "Daddy go," "Go car," or similar combinations.

*(d.) Parts of speech (24–30 months):* Inquire concerning the use of pronouns. Ask what child calls self—by name or "I" or "Me." Also ask if he ever uses the past tense or plural forms.

## SIGNIFICANCE OF EARLY SPEECH

One finds a very wide variability in the size of vocabulary among normal children within this age range. Our norms represent only an average response, and much variation from this is to be expected.

Some children jargon till all of a sudden—but late—they use many words or even word combinations. Others jargon little, and develop their vocabulary slowly but steadily. In general, the expectation is: more jargon than words before 18 months, more words than jargon after that age.

### TABLE 14
### GENETIC SEQUENCE FOR SPEECH DEVELOPMENT

18 months: Ten to twenty words, including names.

21 months: Twenty words (or more), including names. Spontaneous combination of two words. Vocalization consists more of words than of jargon.

24 months: Spontaneous combination of three to four words. Uses pronouns "I," "me," "you," but still more likely to call self by name.

30 months: Uses past tense and plural forms but may still call self by name or "me," rather than "I."

## NAMES OBJECTS (24–30 MONTHS)

This was not included in our testing of current subjects, but is included for the benefit of those testing younger children.

*Procedure:* Show child a penny, key, shoe (the examiner points to his or her own shoe), pencil, knife, and ball. As each is shown, ask, "What's this?" "And what is this?" etc. Repeat as necessary, but do not persist if child cannot respond. Whether or not object is named correctly, ask in each case, "And what do we do with it?" Note whether this question is answered by language or merely by gesture.

TABLE 15
GENETIC SEQUENCE FOR NAMING OBJECTS

24 months: Names two objects.
30 months: Names three objects, and answers at least one "What do we do with it?"

INTERVIEW QUESTIONS (2½–6 YEARS)

The five questions in this section include asking the child his name, age, sex, birthdate, and about his brothers and sisters. Clarity of speech as well as accuracy of information will be of interest to the examiner.

The age of 24 months, so far as the field of language is concerned, is a period of marked transition. Jargon has almost universally dropped out. The speaking vocabulary has shown a sharp increase in its rate of growth.

At 2 years of age, the individual variations in articulation are great, and it is often necessary to call on the parent to interpret the child's response.

The child who does not talk at all is rare by 3 years of age, but there are many whose language is still representative of the more immature stages of 24 and 30 months, particularly in answering questions. Although many 3-year-old children exhibit traces of infantile pronunciation in varying degrees, their speech as a rule is comprehensible. Questioning of the examiner by the child is a much more prominent part of the examination at 3 years than at any earlier age, though it does not reach its peak until 4 years.

The examination of a 4-year-old is an exciting adventure. He talks about everything, plays with words, questions persistently, elaborates simple responses into long narratives, comments with approval on his own behavior and criticizes that of others, balances comparisons. Some speech substitutions occur.

FIVE speaks without infantile articulation. His answers to questions are to the point. Questions are fewer and more relevant than at 4. Language is now essentially complete in structure and form.

*Material:* A list of language questions, as follows; (See Copy Forms Recording Sheet.)

"Tell me your name."
"How old are you?"
"Are you a boy or a girl?"
"When is your birthday?"
"How many brothers and sisters do you have?"

*Procedure:* Ask, "Tell me your name." If the child gives only his first name, ask, "David what?" or "What's the rest of it?" or "What's your other name?"

Ask, "How old are you?" If the child holds up his fingers, ask, "How many is that?" Accept any response given without further question.

Be sure the child's attention is secured and then ask casually (if child is a boy), "Are you a boy or a girl?" If the child is a girl, ask, "Are you a girl or a boy?" If the answer is "No," then ask, "Then what are you?"

Ask, "When is your birthday?" Accept any response given without further questioning. Those children who know the day as well as the month tend to give it spontaneously.

Ask, "How many brothers and sisters do you have?" If child cannot differentiate, ask, "How many brothers? How many sisters?" The siblings' names are usually mentioned spontaneously, but if not, examiner may ask. Children sometimes give names of others who are not their siblings. When this is the case, accept response but do not give credit.

TABLE 16
NORMATIVE RESPONSES TO INTERVIEW QUESTIONS, 2½ to 6 YEARS

NAME: By 2½ years, it is normative for children to give their first name. Failure at this age may be due to negativism or poor attention. Responses may occasionally be difficult to understand because of immature articulation.

At 3 years, most can give first and last name.

AGE: Girls give age in years correctly by 3 years; both sexes by 4 years.

SEX: Girls give sex correctly by 2½ years; both sexes by 3 years. Failure is therefore more significant than success at 4 years, and may be the result of real inability to understand the question or make a distinction, or of inattention or negativism. A tendency to respond to only the last part of the question is an immature form of behavior and makes it essential to follow the prescribed form; that is, it is important to mention the child's actual sex first.

BIRTHDATE: Girls at 3½ are more accurate than boys, but knowing birthday month is not normative until 5½ years. Not till 6½ do they know the day and month of their birthday.

SIBLINGS: Three-and-a-half-year-olds can give the correct number of siblings. Four-and-a-half-year-olds can also give the names of their siblings.

## DISCRIMINATES PREPOSITIONS (3–4 YEARS)

The ease with which the child completes the task required in placing the cube in response to the various preposition commands offers much information as to his maturity level. Can he immediately respond by standing up and placing the cube on, under, behind, in front of, or beside the chair, or does the examiner have to break the direction down into a step-by-step process?

A most important item to record is whether the child is able to physically stay within the task area or quickly leaves to explore the room once he is released from his chair to stand.

A few children cling to the chair and need to remain seated as they place the cube in varying positions. Some refuse to become involved.

*Material:* One-inch cube, one of the ten used for block building, and the chair the child has been seated on. Examiner Recording Sheet.

*Procedure:* Stand up and have the child stand up. Draw the chair to one side. Hand the child the cube and say, "Now put the block *on* the chair."

After he has done this, give the commands for "under," "in back of," "in front of," and "beside" the chair.

If the child each time puts the block on the chair seat but just in different positions, say, "Put the block *on the floor in back of the chair,*" etc.

Complete directions, if necessary, with the suggestion, "Now put the block in my hand"—if the child does not hand it back spontaneously.

*Recording:* The commands to be given are listed at the top of recording sheet. On each dotted line record whether or not the command is obeyed correctly. Place a ( ✔ ) if the preposition is obeyed correctly. If incorrect, place a ( − ) above the line.

*Scoring:* Score the number of prepositions obeyed correctly.

TABLE 17
## AGE NORMS FOR DISCRIMINATES PREPOSITIONS

2 years: Cannot follow through commands involving prepositions.
2½ years: Obeys 1 to 2 prepositions.
3 years: Responds correctly to 3 commands.
3½ years: Responds to 4.
4 years: Succeeds with 5 commands.
4½ to 6 years: Also can follow through with all 5 commands.

## DIGIT REPETITION (3–6 YEARS)

In many ways this test taps an aptitude which is important for successful learning—the child's memory and ability to repeat something said to him. Thus the way in which he responds here is very important to observe.

Failure to repeat the digits correctly may be due to several factors: developmental immaturity, hearing deficiency, lack of number concept, faulty attention, or inadequate auditory imagery.

Certain children, familiar with numbers, translate their auditory experience into visual images. It is common for a child to repeat the numbers under his breath as the examiner gives them, thus reinforcing the auditory impression with speech mechanisms.

Many children below 3½ years have a great deal of difficulty with digit repetition. At 4 years of age, when number concepts are beginning to develop, digit repetition begins to take on meaning for the child.

*Material:* Recording sheet which lists numbers to be tried, as follows:

| | | |
|---|---|---|
| 6 4 1 | 3 5 2 | 8 3 7 |
| 4 7 2 9 | 3 8 5 2 | 7 2 6 1 |
| 2 1 8 5 9 | 4 8 3 7 2 | 9 6 1 8 3 |
| 2 9 4 8 1 6 | 9 6 2 9 3 8 | 5 1 7 2 6 9 |

*Procedure:* Say, "I'm going to say some numbers and when I am through, I want you to say them after me. Listen carefully." Examiner then says, "6 4 1." If no response, or the child responds incorrectly, examiner says again, "6 4 1. Now *you* say 6 4 1."

Continue presenting the groups of numbers, starting with the three digits (give all three sets of three digits) and then continuing with the longer series, until the child fails two of any three sets (that is, fails two threes, two fours, etc).

*General Directions:* Give at the rate of about one numeral per second.

*Recording:* Use a check mark (✔) to indicate that a series was completed correctly. Use a minus sign (−) to indicate an incorrect repetition.

*Scoring:* Indicate the longest series repeated correctly, that is, three, four, five, etc., and number of correct repetitions.

### TABLE 18
### AGE NORMS FOR DIGIT REPETITION

3 years: Repeats 3 (1 of 3 trials).
3½ years: Repeats 3 (2 of 3 trials).
4 years: Repeats 3 (3 of 3 trials).
4½ years: Repeats 4 (2 of 3 trials).
5½ years: Repeats 4 (3 of 3 trials).
6 years: Repeats 5 (1 of 3 trials).

## PICTURE VOCABULARY (2–6 YEARS)

Vocabulary has long been considered one of the best clues to intelligence. Though we ourselves have no specific data to confirm this relationship, we do consider the Picture Vocabulary to be an extremely effective test. It is easy to give and easy for most children to respond to.

*Material:* Examiner—Recording sheet. Child—Eighteen cards in a ringed booklet.

*Procedure:* Show the child the first picture (the airplane). Say, "What's this a picture of?" If the child refuses or gives an incorrect answer, say, "It's an airplane, isn't it?" Then turn to the next card. (Give this help only for the first card.)

*General Directions:* Accept any response given. If the child refuses to respond to any of the first three cards, discontinue the task. But if he gives a response to any one of the first three, present all cards, even if he does not name some correctly, or frequently says, "I don't know."

If the child asks the examiner what a picture is, respond with, "What does it look like to you?" If he does not answer *your* question, answer his question by saying, "That's a foot," etc., and go on to the next card.

*Recording:* Record verbatim the child's name of or response to each picture.

*Scoring:* Score the number of pictures identified correctly.

Score fairly strictly, following Terman's practice. The child *must be able to produce a correct name,* not just show that he knows what the object is. Plurals may be accepted.

*Following are common types of response considered incorrect:*
  (a) Naming part for whole, as hand for arm, toes for foot.
  (b) Naming whole for part, as leg for foot, body for arm.
  (c) Response in terms of use or description, even if correct, as "Thing that locks the door" for key; "What you cut with" for knife.
  (d) Overinclusive concepts, as plant for tree, part of body for arm.

## SCORING STANDARDS FOR PICTURE VOCABULARY

1. Airplane    Correct:   Plane, jet, flying machine
                  Incorrect: Helicopter, air car, ship

2. Telephone   Correct:   Telephone, phone
                  Incorrect: Hello, talk on it

3. Hat    Correct:   Hat, straw hat
                  Incorrect: Cap, thing for your head, dish

4. Ball    Correct:   Baseball, tennis ball, basketball
                  Incorrect: Football, balloon, circle

5. Tree    Correct:   Tree, maple tree, elm tree, etc.
                  Incorrect: Leaf, plant, flower, Christmas tree

6. Key    Correct:   Key lock, key
                  Incorrect: Lock, door locker

7. Horse    Correct:   Horse, pony, horsie
                  Incorrect: Donkey, mule, cow

8. Knife    Correct:   Butcher knife, butter knife, knife
                  Incorrect: Cutter, puts jelly on bread

9. Jacket    Correct:   Coat, jacket
                  Incorrect: Suit, shirt, overcoat, clothes

10. Boat    Correct:   Boat, ship, steamer, ferry, steamship, yacht
                  Incorrect: Boathouse, sailboat

11. Umbrella   Correct:   Umbrella, parasol
                  Incorrect: Rain thing, for the rain, cane

12. Foot    Correct:   Foot, feet, feetsies, foot and toes
                  Incorrect: Shoe, toe, leg, piggies, part of your leg, part of your body

13. Flag    Correct:   Flag, American flag, flagpole, banner, Star Spangled Banner
                  Incorrect: Pole, stick, post

14. Cane          Correct:    Cane, stick, walking stick, candy cane, crook
                  Incorrect: Part of an umbrella, thing you walk with, walker,
                             hooker

15. Arm           Correct:    Arm, arm and hand and shoulder, hand and arm
                  Incorrect: Shoulder, hand, fist, muscle, elbow, he's going to fight

16. Jackknife     Correct:    Pocketknife, knife, jackknife, folding knife, Scout knife
                  Incorrect: Two knives, thing that cuts, table knife

17. Pitcher       Correct:    Pitcher, cream jug, creamer, milk jug
                  Incorrect: Mug, cup, milk, orange juice, pot, coffee pot, drink,
                             bottle, glass, milk bottle

18. Leaf          Correct:    Leaf, maple leaf, tree leaf, leaf of a plant
                  Incorrect: Tree, flower, plant


TABLE 19
AGE NORMS FOR PICTURE VOCABULARY:
NUMBER OF CORRECT RESPONSES

2 years: 2+
2½ years: 7
3 years: 11
3½ years: 12
4 years: 14
5 years: 15
6 years: 16


## COMPREHENSION QUESTIONS (3–6 YEARS)

The ability to understand and answer these seemingly simple questions is rarely found below 3 years of age, and is still not present in many children of that age. Group A, "What must you do when you are hungry, sleepy, or cold?" elicits varied and specific responses from 3-year-olds, but most children at this age get only one correct. By 4½, most get all three correct.

Group B, "What must you do when you have lost something?" and "What must you do before you cross the street?" creates difficulty for the 3-year-old. It is the 4- and 5-year-olds who can understand the social implications of these questions, and by 5 both sets of questions are answered correctly.

### WHAT MUST YOU DO?

*Material:* Recording sheet listing three questions (Group A) and two questions (Group B) as follows:

GROUP A:

"What must you do when you are hungry?"

"What must you do when you are sleepy?"

"What must you do when you are cold?"

GROUP B:

"What must you do when you have lost something?"

"What must you do before you cross the street?"

*Procedure:* Ask the questions verbatim. Some small children do not understand "must." When this seems to be the cause of failure, the question may be repeated, using the form, "What *do* you do . . .?" Otherwise, the form should not be changed. But when a response has been obtained, supplementary questions may be asked, if necessary, to clarify the answer. The examiner may ask, "What do you mean by that?" Do not pursue the questioning beyond this.

*Scoring:* For questions in Group A, the examiner uses her judgment as to whether or not the response is or is not satisfactory.

For questions in Group B, the following clues may be used in scoring: Correct responses to "lost something" should refer to search: "Hunt for it," "Find it," "Ask my mommy to help look for it," etc. "Get another" is less directly responsive to the main implication of the question and is counted as a failure. Some children will answer, "Find a policeman," indicating that the question has been misunderstood. In such cases, say, "Yes, that's right. And what must you do when you have lost something that belongs to you?" Failures include such answers as "Cry," "Get a spanking," "Nothing."

For the second question, "Cross the street," the answer should suggest caution or conformity with regulations in crossing the street: "Look out for the cars," "Wait for the light," "Take my mommy's hand," "Look up and down." Failures include: "Run," "Hurry up," "Get a spanking," etc.

Misunderstanding of the question is sometimes indicated by a child who has been conditioned against crossing the street while playing. He may reply: "Don't cross the street," "Don't go into the street." In such cases the question may be rephrased: "If you're out for a walk with your mother and come to the corner, what must you do before you go across the street?"

## Rules For Scoring

### COMPREHENSION QUESTIONS A

*Hungry:* Nearly any food response is acceptable: "Eat," "Candy," "Drink of milk," "Supper." Or more elaborately: "Eat my supper" or "Wait for supper."

Not acceptable: "Tell Mommy" or any similar response.

*Sleepy:* "Sleep," "Rest," "Bed," "Nap," "Close eyes," "Grandma tucks me in," "Mommy puts me to bed," "Go to bed," etc. All are acceptable.
Not acceptable: "Tell Mommy," "Yawn," "Get up," "Get off my bed," "You're tired."

*Cold:* Anything to imply getting warm: "Go into house," "Put on coat," "Put on blanket," "Get sweater," "Get dressed." Or just "Coat." Or, "Close the door." Or any response related to stove or heater.
Not acceptable: "Get warm" (since this is not specific enough). Or "I got a cold," "I sick," "I blew my nose," "Freeze," "Have a doctor," "Have some medicine."

### COMPREHENSION QUESTIONS B

*Lost something:* Any answer is acceptable which refers to search, to looking around, to getting help in finding the thing. Thus: "Hunt for it," "Find it," "Get a new one."
Not acceptable: "Tell Mommy," "Cry," "Get a spanking."

*Before you cross the street:* Acceptable answers include: "Look out for cars," "Look both ways," "Wait for light," "Take Mommy's hand," "Stop," "Ask policeman."
Not acceptable: "Run," "Hurry," "Walk."

### TABLE 20
### NORMS FOR RESPONSE TO COMPREHENSION QUESTIONS

COMPREHENSION QUESTIONS A:

    3 years: Answers one correctly.
    3½ years: Answers two correctly.
    4 years: Answers three correctly.

COMPREHENSION QUESTIONS B:

    4 years: Answers one correctly.
    5 years: Answers two correctly.

## ACTION AGENT (2½–6 YEARS)

We have through the years found this to be one of the most effective of our language tests. It is easy to give and to record and, if the child is up to it, well received. If the child is not up to it, failure is clearly observed by the examiner but, presuming the child cooperates at all, failure is not obvious or discouraging to him or her. Thus the child, even when quite fully inaccurate, is not himself disturbed, and failure does not disturb the flow of the examination.

*Material:* Recording sheet which lists the following questions, including the initial questions which are not scored. The initial questions are "What runs?" and "What cries?"

The questions to be scored are:

| | |
|---|---|
| 1. What scratches? | 11. What sails? |
| 2. What sleeps? | 12. What boils? |
| 3. What flies? | 13. What floats? |
| 4. What bites? | 14. What growls? |
| 5. What swims? | 15. What stings? |
| 6. What burns? | 16. What gallops? |
| 7. What cuts? | 17. What aches? |
| 8. What blows? | 18. What explodes? |
| 9. What shoots? | 19. What roars? |
| 10. What melts? | 20. What mews? |

*Procedure:* Secure the child's attention and ask, "What runs?" "Tell me something that runs." It may be necessary to repeat the question, but do not persist too long. If no response or an inappropriate one is given, say, "A car runs, doesn't it? And horses run, too." (Avoid an example such as "Boys and girls" which is appropriate to several of the next few questions, in order not to set up a perseverative response with doubtful comprehension.) Pause briefly and then ask, "What cries? Tell me something that cries." Again, if the response is unsatisfactory, answer the question yourself. Then proceed with the test proper, without supplying any more answers. If a good response is given to the first sample question, it is often unnecessary to provide an answer to the second question.

*General Directions:* Precede each question with the word "What?" Present all the questions even though the child may frequently give an "I don't know" answer. However, if the child fails or refuses to respond to the first three or four questions, discontinue the test.

*Scoring:* Accept any response given without question, but scoring should be highly discriminating. The accompanying list of scoring standards should be useful in determining the acceptability or nonacceptability of responses. Successful responses according to Stutsman are those which name:

1. The agent performing the act;
2. The direct object, as "paper cuts";
3. Unusual responses with logical association.

Perseverative responses must be scored as successes if they are discriminatingly used, otherwise they are usually failures, even though appropriate to some of the questions to which they are given. Thus "Baby" may be reported as scratching, sleeping, biting, and if a more appropriate response is given to the intervening "What flies?" and other questions, all of these are correct. If, however, the perseverative response is given to more than one inappropriate question as well, *all should be counted as failures.*

Record with a check mark (✔) correct answers. Record child's response verbatim when an incorrect response is given and mark with a minus sign (−).

## ACTION AGENT:
## SCORING STANDARDS

RUNS:     Acceptable: Cars, trains, motorcycles, etc., clock, water, people, animals, leg, feet, furnace.
    Unacceptable: Electricity, batteries.

CRIES:     Acceptable: People, eyes.
    Unacceptable: Animals.

SCRATCHES: Acceptable: People, some animals as kitten, tiger, fingers, fingernails, me, dogs, scratchy things, prickers, hand. Or object (car, backs, leg).
    Unacceptable: Itches, mosquito bites, saw.

SLEEPS:     Acceptable: People, animals, eyes, "That's when you dream," dolls.
    Unacceptable: In bed, "When you're sleepy," tired, yawns.

FLIES:     Acceptable: Birds, fly, butterflies, bees, airplanes, helicopters, kites.
    Unacceptable: Paper.

BITES:     Acceptable: People, animals, bugs, my brother, bad things, teeth, bee, mosquitoes, cats.
    Unacceptable: Birdies, rabbits, jellyfish, whale.

SWIMS:     Acceptable: Fish, man, people, frog, dog, turtles.
    Unacceptable: Boats.

BURNS:     Acceptable: Fire, matches, fireplace, food, house, stove, oven, rubbish.
    Unacceptable: Fire engine, people, pot.

CUTS:     Acceptable: Knife, scissors, saw, ax, etc. Or object, as paper, board, bread, fingers, tree, me, people.
    Unacceptable: Chairs, cat.

BLOWS:     Acceptable: Wind, person, air, balloon, horn, mouth, trees, nose.
    Unacceptable: Train, chimney.

SHOOTS:     Acceptable: People, guns, pistols, bullets, arrows, airplane.
    Unacceptable: Bombs.

MELTS:      Acceptable: Ice cream, ice, snow, butter, candle, candy, wax, or (the agent) sun, heat.
            Unacceptable: Water, babies.

SAILS:      Acceptable: Boat, ship, sailboat, sailor.
            Unacceptable: Animals.

BOILS:      Acceptable: Kettle, many kinds of food or liquid.
            Unacceptable: Stove, teapot, pancake.

FLOATS:     Acceptable: Boats, wood, fish, sticks, ducks, paper, balloon, washcloth, soap.
            Unacceptable: River, fire, water, rain.

GROWLS:     Acceptable: Dog, wolf, tiger, bear, monster, "My father when he's mad."
            Unacceptable: Lion, cat, people, flowers, owls.

STINGS:     Acceptable: Bee, fly, wasp, mosquito, bug, jellyfish, pricker, smoke (in eyes), finger.
            Unacceptable: Rats, cow, butterfly; any confusion with "stinks."

GALLOPS:    Acceptable: Horse, pony, animals, people, feet, or "I do."
            Unacceptable: Kitty, cow.

ACHES:      Acceptable: Ear or earache, tooth or toothache, various parts of body, pain.
            Unacceptable: Baby, man, eggs.

EXPLODES:   Acceptable: Firecrackers, gun, cannon, gasoline, dynamite, bomb, houses, ship.
            Unacceptable: Fire, metal.

ROARS:      Acceptable: Lion, wind, airplane, engine, train, car, monster, cannons, "My daddy when he's angry."
            Unacceptable: Bear, bull, tiger.

MEWS:       Acceptable: Cat, kitty.
            Unacceptable: Other animals, music, fiddle.

## TABLE 21
### NORMS FOR ACTION AGENT QUESTIONS

2½ years: 3 correct.
3 years: 6–7 correct.
3½ years: 12 correct.
4 years: 14 correct.
4½ years: 16 correct.
5 years: 17 correct.
5½ years: 18–19 correct.
6 years: 19 correct.

# 7

## Personal-Social Behavior *

The term personal-social has proved to be a very useful one in describing not only the child's ways of responding in social situations but also his individual and characteristic manner of responding in all situations. Personal-social behavior includes not only primarily social behavior, but also the kinds of behavior which characterize personality. Actually much personal-social behavior is essentially personal rather than social.

The behavior we term personal-social does not have to be isolated to be observed. It is in evidence whenever we have a child responding to any situation whatever. We see it in motor, language, and adaptive behavior; we see it in the home, in the nursery school, and on the street. Within its scope are items which have a much wider range of occurrence than in any other field.

In studying the personal-social behavior of the individual, we find first a need for generalized age norms. In spite of wide individual variations in behavior, very specific age characteristics may be observed. These age characteristics, when arranged in genetic gradation, outline developmental trends which are common to most children and which largely determine the course that behavior will follow with increasing maturity.

Such normal and usual patterns of development may be used as guideposts of comparison in studying the individual child, but it is the flow of the developing pattern which helps us to know a child dynamically.

*Once we have familiarized ourselves with normatively typical*

* This chapter is reproduced, with some revisions, from *The First Five Years of Life*, with the authors' permission.

*modes of development, we are in a position to weigh fairly the individual child's deviations of behavior and to interpret the flow or trend of his individual developmental pattern.*

One child may consistently exhibit wide swings of behavior from one extreme to another. He may, for instance, attain an unusually early proficiency in a certain behavior only to lose it at a more advanced age. For example, he may lace his shoes at 2 years and yet ask for help at 4. Or he may lag far behind the norm and then suddenly perform in a manner fully up to or even above his age level.

He may refuse to lie on his stomach until 10 months of age and then suddenly begin to creep—and creep practically as well as a 10-month-old child who has been creeping for a month or more. He may have an extremely poor appetite up to 2 years and then suddenly develop a ravenous appetite. He may consistently wet his bed at night until 3½ years and then suddenly have a dry bed and never return to wetting.

A child with wide swings of behavior in one field will probably have wide swings of behavior in all fields. That is the way he develops, and what appears to be an inconsistency in development is actually consistent for him. Such a seemingly erratic course is more clearly understood when it can be matched against some normative type of pattern around which it varies.

At certain ages these swings from one extreme to another may be very wide and yet remain normal. For instance at 2½ years, it is quite normal for a child to vary between the two poles of aggression and withdrawal. Part of his behavior is marked by extremely aggressive tendencies such as grabbing and refusing to comply, while at other times he will be very withdrawn and will yield much too easily. A child whose typical style of development is to swing from one extreme to another may be expected to exaggerate these normal 2½-year-old swings. The exaggeration may be so marked and may lead to such inconsistencies of behavior as to give the false impression that the specific environmental situation and not the child's developmental status is determining behavior.

A clear understanding of the more basic kinds of behavior also makes possible a realization that what is deemed a failure at one age level may actually be a more advanced stage than an earlier "success." Training which was apparently successful at one age level may no longer be successful at a succeeding age level. Very often babies who have been "trained" to the toilet for their bowel movements up to one year of age suddenly resist the toilet and have their daily movements at irregular times. The mother may feel ineffectual, or she may try to force the child to comply with her wishes since he has complied before. Actually the child is acquiring voluntary sphincter control and his "failure" is due to sphincter contraction. Voluntary sphincter contraction precedes voluntary sphincter release and later becomes associated with the child's ability to verbalize his sensations so that he may reach the toilet before he relaxes the sphincter.

In no other fields are the ups and downs, the progressions and regressions so clearly seen as in the personal-social. Since the requisite neurological structure is more complex, it is therefore more subject to deterioration under stress. How often do we see regressions in elimination, eating, or dressing when a new baby comes into the family, depending upon which ability is the most recently acquired?

The personal-social behavior of the preschool child clearly does not depend on himself alone; it is sensitive to environmental influences. Like postural behavior, developing personal-social behavior follows a basic maturational sequence, but it does need guidance. Since it is usually the child's mother who is his guide during the early years, it becomes extremely important for her to have a knowledge of the general route along which he is traveling.

It is almost as if the child's nervous system were completed by his mother, her part being that she must think ahead for the child. If she has in mind a preview of the normative sequence through which a behavior is likely to develop, she is in a position to foresee and to interpret the developing behavior in all its variations. She may know why the child behaves as he does and she will know better what to expect next. She will not try to make him do too much by himself. Since she knows at what stage he is, she can supply the first and second steps of a given behavior and then let him supply the third step (which he might not have been able to do unless she had supplied the first two). For instance, he may not be ready to put toys away on command, but if his mother hands him a toy, he can put it away. The tension felt by a mother who requires too much of a child because she does not know what to expect and cannot see a single bit of behavior in its true perspective may actually cause the child's behavior to be less effective than it might have been.

One important principle which a mother should keep in mind is that the child, in much of his behavior, seems to learn backward rather than forward. He undresses before he dresses, takes a bit of food out of his mouth before he can put it in, has to understand puddles before he can stop making them, empties the wastebasket before he fills it. It is only gradually that the child's interest in the ends of things gives way to an interest in their beginnings as well. As he gets older, he responds to more and more of a situation until finally he can carry through a whole process unaided.

Some of the more characteristic age sequences in the patterning of personal-social behavior described in this chapter include eating, sleeping, elimination, dressing, communication, play, aesthetic behavior, and "out-for-a-walk" behavior.

It is of course apparent that some personal-social behaviors evidenced in everyday situations depend to a large extent on home training. Even in such cases the developmental concept is important, inasmuch as the training could never have been successful unless the organism was ready to be trained. However, since the child may be taught many personal-social behavior "tricks" some time before he would have exhibited them without coaching, the early appearance of any one of the listed behaviors is not in itself an indication of precocity or superiority.

On the other hand, the items in our normative sequences are placed late enough so that it is fair to say that a child who has not attained any one of them, with or without training, at the age indicated, is slow so far as that item is concerned. However, all age placements are approximate. The genetic sequences are offered as examples of typical trends and of sequence order. For the reasons just explained, *liberal allowance must be made for normal individual variations.*

### TABLE 22
### EATING BEHAVIOR

#### SELF-FEEDING (CUP)

18 months—Lifts cup to mouth and drinks well.

             Hands empty cup to mother; if she is not there to take it, may drop it.

21 months—Handles cup well: lifting, drinking, and replacing on tray.

24 months—Holds small glass in one hand as drinks.

36 months—Pours well from a pitcher.

#### SELF-FEEDING (SPOON)

18 months—Fills spoon.

             Experiences difficulty in inserting spoon into mouth; apt to turn it in mouth.

             Considerable spilling.

24 months—Inserts spoon in mouth without turning.
Moderate spilling.
36 months—Girls may have supinate grasp of spoon.
Little spilling.

GENERAL RESPONSE TO MEALS

18 months—Hands empty dishes to mother.
24 months—Continues to need help in feeding.
Is apt to dawdle and play with food, especially stirring it.
Refuses disliked foods.
Very little conversation with meals.
36 months—Rarely needs assistance to complete a meal.
Interested in setting table.
Either talks or eats.
42 months—Child "can," but "won't." Good at self-help if so inclined.
May object to kinds of food provided and the way they are served.
48 months—Good at helping set table.
May wish to choose own menu.
Can combine talking and eating.
Likes to serve self.
Much getting up from table, especially for toileting.
60 months—Eats rapidly.
Very social and talkative during meal.
Seldom gets up from table.

The preceding sequences do not give a complete picture of eating behavior, but they do suggest the main trends. Individual differences stand out very clearly in relation to eating. Appetite, response to taste, sight, smell, consistency, and color, as well as response to new foods, all play a specific role. Appetite sometimes seems to follow a definite curve, with the lowest point between 15 and 18 months; while at 30 months appetite may fluctuate from extreme hunger to none at all. Comparable swings may be noted in other fields of behavior at this age.

Feeding difficulties, when chronic, have usually been present from birth or soon after. Children suffering from such difficulties are peculiarly sensitive to the eating situation. They may refuse to eat when anyone other than their mother is in the room, they gag at the slightest lump even up to 4 years of age, or they vomit when they see others eating. Something more fundamental than management lies at the basis of such serious feeding problems. Fortunately, with proper handling, most tend to improve with age.

In ordinary cases, management has much to do with the success or failure of eating. Many difficulties arise between 15 and 24 months because insufficient participation in the meal is allowed. On the other hand, at 24 and even at 36 months difficulties may arise because too much is expected of the child. Feeding the child with no one else in the room, filling his spoon for him without feeding him, giving him his meals in courses, confining him to a high chair if he is difficult to keep at the table, allowing him to eat by himself and to call out when he is finished, permitting him to choose his menus—these and many other factors may greatly influence the success or failure of eating. It is especially important for parents not to show that they care terribly what or how much the child eats. Even a very young child can easily get the upper hand of parents who show too great concern.

The child gives cues as to his capacities and idiosyncrasies all along the way. It is up to the adult to be alert to these cues and to respect the child's appetites and desires. With knowledge beforehand of the way in which feeding behavior ordinarily matures, it is possible to strike a balance between the child's preparedness and the demands made upon him.

### TABLE 23
### SLEEPING BEHAVIOR

NAP

15 months—Usually has one nap a day, which has shifted from late A.M. to early P.M.

36 months—Nap is beginning to disappear, though child rests or plays in bed without resistance.

If he goes to sleep, has at least an hour's nap.

48 months—Nap is definitely going out, but 36-month patterns still persist.

May begin to resist resting in bed.

60 months—Nap is rare.

GOING TO BED: EITHER NAP OR NIGHT SLEEP

15 months—Put to bed easily.

18 months—Difficulties may arise when leaving child. He may cry for mother to be with him.

Lying down beside child or sitting next to crib usually induces sleep.

21 months—Does not go to sleep at once.

Keeps demanding things, such as a drink, food, or the toilet before going off to sleep. This is more common at night.

24 months—Demands to take toys, such as teddy bear or rubber car, to bed with him. Much calling back of mother for another drink of water, kiss, handkerchief, toileting.

30 months—Prolongs process of going to bed by setting up a complicated ritual which must be rigidly adhered to.

36 months—Less dependent on taking toys to bed with him.
48 months—Tries to put off starting to go to bed.
  Rarely takes things to bed with him.

### DURING SLEEP

18 months—May awaken during the night crying. This is often associated with wetting the bed.
21 months—May awaken crying or may ask to go to the toilet.
24 months—Usually responds without fussing to being taken up to go to the toilet in the evening. Is half asleep when taken up.
36 months—Beginning to sleep through the night without wetting or having to be picked up.
48 months—Sleeps through the night without having to get up to urinate.
  May awaken crying from a dream and can usually tell dreams.
60 months—Quieter during sleep.

Sleeping may be one of the easiest aspects of the child's life to manage; or it may be the most difficult. Many problems arise because the child is put to bed too early or is expected to take a nap when he wishes only to rest. The child is usually the winner in any battles which occur, and it is unfortunate that he is not more frequently met halfway, for when he is so met, he is much less demanding.

The preceding sequences have touched upon the more common difficulties in going to bed, the occasion when most sleep problems occur. But there are many other forms of presleep adjustment which show how difficult it often is for the child to release consciousness. Various methods to which he resorts to bring about this release are singing, talking, head rolling, head banging, and thumb sucking. Each of these follows its own sequence until it is no longer needed.

It is the emotionally dependent child who presents the most difficulties in relation to sleep. As late as 4 years, he may verbalize to himself during the day that he is a big boy, but at night he is only a little boy. He has difficulty in falling asleep unless his mother is in the room, and if he awakes during the night he wants to crawl into his mother's bed. No one can put him to bed but his mother and no one can care for him when he wakes up but his mother, not even his father. Drastic handling does not improve his sleeping behavior and only increases his dependence upon his mother. A slow separation can be planned for and executed as the child seems ready, but usually he cannot make the adjustment without adult help and planning.

## TABLE 24
## ELIMINATION

15 months—Cooperative toilet response, especially for bowel movement.
Indicates wet pants or puddles, usually by pointing.
May awake dry from nap.

18 months—Toilet regulated for both bowel and bladder control.
May awaken at night and cry to be changed.

21 months—Beginning to tell needs of toilet and usually uses same word for both functions.
Increased frequency of urinating.

24 months—Verbally differentiates bowel and bladder functions but is not dependable.

30 months—Longer periods between eliminations.
May show resistance to toilet if taken too frequently.
Some may be considered "trained."

36 months—Takes responsibility for toilet himself, but always tells that he is going.
Is apt to hold off too long, dances up and down, and just begins to wet pants before he reaches toilet.
Able to go by self but needs help on back buttons.
Attempts to wipe self not very successful.
May verbalize difference between boys and girls in that girls sit down but boys stand up to go to the toilet.
Some girls may attempt to urinate standing up in imitation of boys.
May be dry at night without being taken up.

48 months—Goes by self and can manage clothes without difficulty.
May still tell before he goes, but insists on going by self and often prefers to have bathroom door shut.
Wants privacy for self, but likes to go into bathroom when others are there.
Marked interest in bathrooms in other people's houses.
May show excessive interest in bowel movements, and asks many questions about humans and animals in relation to this function.

60 months—Takes complete charge of self, including wiping.
Does not mention to adult that he is going to the toilet.
Becoming self-conscious about exposing self.
May show a silly response about going to the toilet.

A much earlier (1930s) tendency to train a baby for elimination as early as 8 to 36 weeks of age is giving way to a new understanding of the manner in which a child achieves control. The "successes" of early training were often transient and superficial and not worth the excessive amount of time needed to achieve them. True training takes time and requires that the child will have achieved a certain level of physiological readiness.

Consider, for instance, bowel control. There is often a successful response to training right after meals in the earliest months. (Before that the bowel movement may have occurred during the meal.) After 4 to 6 months this close relationship of eating and eliminating no longer holds, and the time of elimination tends to become very irregular.

Around 8 to 9 months a similar relationship may again be set up after one or possibly two meals, and the child may appear to be definitely trained at 1 year of age, only to repeat his former lapses as he grows older.

And so it goes. The course from 15 months to 2 years of age is not a steady one. The time of the movement shifts, the toilet may be resisted, and occasional accidents occur up to 2 years. Accidents are relatively rare after this age, but a new complication may arise at 27 to 30 months when the child withholds bowel movements for as long as two or three days, and constipation may set in. This withholding is an exercise and expression of increasing bowel control.

In a similar way bladder control is attained. Nowadays most parents wait until the child is at least 2 years old before making vigorous efforts at any kind of toilet training.

The verbal tie-up with elimination is very significant in that it can tell what stage in development the child has reached. Here as in other behaviors he seems to learn backward. At first he is able only to point out a puddle or wet pants. Later he can "tell" verbally during the act. Finally he tells before the act. A child who is just beginning to indicate wet or soiled pants at 2½ years instead of at the usual 18 to 24 months has still a long way to go before he is "trained." The words "bathroom" or "toilet" may mean little or nothing to the young child. Simple words that concretely express the function of elimination are more effective for helping him establish control.

TABLE 25
DRESSING

15 months—Cooperates in dressing by extending arm or leg.
18 months—Can take off mittens, hat, and socks.
　　　　　　Can unzip zippers.
　　　　　　Tries to put on shoes.
24 months—Can remove shoes if laces are untied.
　　　　　　Helps in getting dressed—finds large armholes and thrusts his arms into them.

Helps pull up or push down panties.

Washes hands and dries them, but does neither very well.

36 months—Greater interest and ability in undressing. May need some assistance with shirts and sweaters.

Is able to unbutton all front and side buttons by pushing buttons through buttonholes.

In dressing does not know back from front. Apt to put pants on backward, has difficulty in turning socks to get heels on in back.

Puts shoes on but may put them on wrong feet.

Intent on lacing shoes, but usually laces them incorrectly.

Washes and dries hands.

Brushes teeth with supervision.

48 months—Is able to undress and dress himself with little assistance.

Distinguishes between front and back of clothes and puts them on correctly.

Washes and dries hands and face.

Brushes teeth.

60 months—Undresses and dresses with care.

May be able to tie shoelaces (usually at 6 years).

Children's clothes have indeed been simplified within the past few years so that the child not only tries to cooperate in dressing but can actually do many things for himself long before he could do so with more complicated clothing. This fact tends to make us err on the side of expecting too much from the young child. Dressing is so intimately bound up with motor coordination that we should attempt to measure just how much the child can do for himself and not expect him to do more.

In dressing behavior we see a marked sex difference. Girls dress themselves much more efficiently and earlier than boys, due to a better fine motor coordination and especially a more flexible rotation at the wrist. Some girls at 2 and 3 years dress themselves so skillfully that they may dress and undress just for fun, while at the other extreme boys of 5 and 6 years may still have difficulty in buttoning buttons and dressing in general. The poor wrist rotation of the boys may also be observed in handwashing, when they are unable to get the customary rotary movement but instead rub the two palmar surfaces together. This is also evident in their inability to turn a doorknob far enough to open a door.

The early dresser is difficult to manage because he (or she) will not allow any help though he still needs it, while the late dresser needs help long after the mother wishes that he were dressing himself.

TABLE 26
COMMUNICATION

18 months—Communicates both by gestures and words, but words are beginning to replace gestures.

Responds to simple commands.

Verbalizes ends of actions such as "Bye-bye," "Thank you," "All gone."

Refusals may be expressed by "No," but more usually by bodily response.

21 months—Asks for food, toilet, drink.

Repeats single words said to him, or last word or two of a phrase.

24 months—Speech accompaniment of activity.

Asks questions such as "What's that?"

Verbalizes immediate experiences.

Much vocalization in a group, but little conversation.

Refers to himself by his name.

Refusals expressed by "No."

30 months—Demands to do things by himself though he may not be able to.

May repeat everything said to him. (This type of child has difficulty in comprehending what is asked of him.)

Gives his full name.

Refers to himself by pronoun rather than by name.

Elicits attention of adult: "Look at me."

May say "No" when he means "Yes."

36 months—Interest in conforming expressed by "Do it this way?"

Expresses desires verbally: "I can do it all by myself" or "I want to do so and so."

May ask for help especially from mother though he may be capable of doing what he is asking to be helped in.

Asks questions rhetorically.

Expresses limitations by "I don't know" or may quickly change the subject.

Expresses refusals by "I don't want to" more often than by "No."

48 months—Can carry on long, involved conversations.

Reasoning more complicated—figuring things out for himself.

Can tell a story which may be a mixture of real and unreal.

Precedes sentences with interjections such as "Oh," "Hey," "Ooh," and "Yes, sir."

Demands detailed explanations, often asks "Why?" until adult is unable to answer.

Interest in things being funny: "Wouldn't it be funny to ride on a broken bus!"

Lavish use of the word *everything,* such as "I know everything." Apt to end a sentence with "and everything."

Tendency toward self-praise: "I'm smart." "I have good ideas, don't I?"

Bosses and criticizes others.

Calls people names: "You're a rat."

Elicits attention of adult to specific abilities with such remarks as, "Wanna see me?"

Does not like to admit inability and covers it up by saying, "I will do it a little different." May become angry at failure and say, "I'll sock you in the jaw" or "I'm mad."

Refusals previously expressed by "No" and "I don't want to" may be superseded by "I won't."

60 months—Can tell a long story accurately.

May keep adding and adding to reality making it more and more fantastic.

Polite and tactful in speech. When asked to do something says, "Sure." If the task is too hard, may say, "I don't know how to do hard ones."

Everything is "easy" even before he has attempted a task.

Asks many questions about how things work, what things are for, and the meaning of words.

Communicative behavior is an extremely significant category of personal-social behavior for without communication of some sort it would indeed be difficult for the child to manifest many forms of personal-social behavior. In spite of this significance, relatively little is known of one of the most important aspects of language behavior, namely, the verbal equipment of the child in the way of understanding. We do not know as much as we should about what the child really understands. Long before many parents cease to talk about the child in his presence, he is well aware of what is being said, in general purport, if not in detail. At older ages we find that the verbal approach to the child is by far the quickest and most effective, provided he is contacted at the right maturity level. Often the right word or phrase can bring release from a difficult situation. "You *could* give it back to him," allows the 2½-year-old to return a plaything without loss of face. Greater efforts to utilize a verbal approach based upon the child's increasing powers of understanding will result in more harmonious personal-social relations. More precise insights into the purely developmental aspects of language comprehension could vastly improve our methods of child care. Here again the significance of the developmental point of view asserts itself.

TABLE 27
GENERAL PLAY ACTIVITIES

15 months—Endless exercise of walking activities.

Throws and picks up objects and throws again.

Puts one object after another in and out of receptacles.

18 months—Very rapid shifts in attention especially expressed by gross motor shifts. Moves actively from place to place and "gets into" everything.

Pulls toy.

Carries or hugs doll or teddy bear.

Imitates many things such as reading newspaper, sweeping, dusting.

Solitary or onlooker play.

24 months—Less rapid shifts in attention. Interest in dawdling and manipulating play material to feel, pat, and pound.

Interest in dolls and teddy bears (domestic mimicry); beads (strings them or drops them in holes in tops of boxes or cans only to dump them out and repeat the process); blocks and wagon (transports blocks in wagon more than building with them).

Does not imitate things remembered, but only those events which are present to his senses.

Parallel play predominates when with other children, though he obviously enjoys being with other children.

Little interest in what other children do or say, but may hug them or push them out of the way as though they were physical objects.

Little social give-and-take but much physical snatch and grab accompanied by defending rights by kicking and pulling hair which may end in hilarious scuffle.

Does not ask for help; adult must be constantly watchful and ready to help without waiting to be asked.

36 months—Dramatization and imagination beginning to enter into play.

Interest in combining playthings such as blocks and cars, making roads, garages, and bridges.

Increasing interest in playing with other children rather than playing alone. May play in groups of two or three, but these are constantly shifting in makeup and activity.

Cooperative activity taking the place of physical contact.

Is willing to wait turn.

Will put away toys with some supervision.

48 months—Considerable increase in constructive use of materials and in manipulation and dramatization of play.

Has very complicated ideas but is unable to carry them out in detail, and has no carry-over from day to day.

Prefers to play in a group of two or three children. Often chooses favorite companion of own sex.

Suggests turns but is often bossy in directing others and is often silly in play and may purposely do things wrong.

Puts away toys by himself.

Marked rise in activity.

Likes to "dress up."

60 months—Very fond of cutting out and pasteing and in working on a specific project such as a store or a boat (project is carried over from day to day), and in dressing up in adults' clothes.

Definite interest in finishing what he has started even though it takes several days.

Plays in groups of two to five. Friendships are becoming stronger.

Spurred on in activity by rivalry.

Interest in going on excursions.

## TABLE 28
## AESTHETIC BEHAVIOR*

18 months—*Painting* Whole arm movements.

Very few strokes on a page, often in the form of an arc.

Shifting of brush from one hand to the other.

Satisfied with only one color.

*Blocks* Carries blocks around the room, pounds them together, or dumps in a mass.

Only building may be a tower of three or four.

*Music* Spontaneous humming or singing of syllables.

Wide range in tone, pitch, and intensity of voice.

Very much aware of sounds such as bells, whistles, clocks.

Rhythmic response to music with whole body activity.

*Pictures, rhymes, and stories* Attends to pictures of familiar objects in books.

Listens to short rhymes with interesting sounds, especially when they are accompanied by action or pictures. Likes to have them sung.

24 months—*Painting* More wrist action than at 18 months.

Less shift in handedness, though often paints with a brush in each hand.

"Scrubbing" paper with little regard for color. Paints several colors over each other vigorously, with muddy effect.

Experimenting with vertical and horizontal lines, dots, and circular movements.

Goes out-of-bounds: painting on table, easel, floor, own hands, other children.

Process, not end result, important to the child.

Easily distracted and does not always watch hand movements.

Social enjoyment of painting on same paper with another child.

*Finger painting* Initial objection to feeling of paint and getting hands dirty, but enjoyment after a few trials.

Rhythmical movements with whole hands.

*Clay* Initial objection to feeling of clay and getting hands dirty, but enjoyment after a few trials.

Manipulates—pounding, squeezing, and pulling off small pieces; often handing to adult.

*The sequences are descriptive of nursery school behavior, and were drawn up by Janet Learned Rodell, former Director of the Gesell Institute Nursery School.

Uses other materials in combination with clay, such as tongue depressors, blocks, cars, and wooden animals.

Often experiments with the taste of clay.

*Sand, stones, water* Fills pails and dishes with sand and stones, dumping and throwing.

High interest in water play—soap bubbles, "painting" with water, sailing boats, and extensive hand washing.

*Blocks* Used manipulatively, filling wagons, dumping, and rolling.

Sometimes used imaginatively as coal, ashes, lumber, etc.

Some building of towers and lines, often combining various sizes of blocks in random order.

*Music* Sings phrases of songs, generally not on pitch.

Recognition of a few melodies.

Enjoyment of rhythmical equipment such as rocking boat, swing, and rocking chair. These often stimulate spontaneous singing.

Rhythmical responses such as bending knees in bouncing motion, swaying, swinging arms, nodding head, and tapping feet.

*Pictures, rhymes, and stories* Enjoyment of simple pictures with few details and clear color.

Interest in rhymes.

Language (of the child) often rhythmical and repetitive.

Attends to short simple stories with repetition and familiar subjects.

*Miscellaneous* Strong tactile sense: likes to touch fur, silk, angora, etc.

Also tastes many objects and materials such as clay, paint, crayon; puts tongue against glass, wood, etc.

Imitation strong at this age.

36 months—*Painting* Strokes more varied and rhythmical.

Beginnings of design emerging.

Often covers whole page with one color, or blocks of various colors.

Sometimes names finished product, but seldom any recognizable resemblance.

Joy and pride in product; exclaims, "Look what I made!"

Works with more concentration and precision.

Dislikes to share paper with others.

*Finger painting* Experimenting with finger movements as well as whole hands.

Some feeling for design.

*Clay* Enjoyment of manipulating with hands, patting, making holes with fingers, and squeezing.

Beginning of form: makes flat round "cakes" and balls; rolls long narrow strips, etc.

Some naming of product with general approximation in shape.

*Sand* Makes cakes, pies, etc.

*Blocks* Order and balance in building.

Combining with cars, trains, etc.

Often names what he is making.

*Music* Many can reproduce whole songs though generally not on pitch.

Beginning to match simple tones.

Less inhibition in joining group singing.

Can recognize several melodies.

Experimenting with musical instruments.

Enjoyment of group participation in rhythms.

Gallop, jump, walk, and run in fairly good time to music.

Enjoy dressing up in costumes for rhythms.

*Stories* Much longer span of interest in listening to stories.

Continued enjoyment of the familiar, with more details and less repetition.

Insists on stories being retold and reread word for word without changes.

48 months—*Painting* Designs and crude letters.

Active imagination with shifting of ideas as painting progresses.

Increase in verbal accompaniment explaining pictures.

Products have personal value to child—wants to take them home.

Holds brush in adult manner.

*Finger painting* Continued experimentation with fingers, hands, and arms in rhythmical manner.

Some representation and naming.

*Clay* Large masses of clay used.

Increase in representation and imagination.

*Blocks* Extensive complicated structures combining many shapes in symmetrical manner.

Little carry-over of interest to following day if structure is left standing.

Cooperation in building in small groups.

*Music* Increase in voice control.

Can play simple singing games.

High interest in dramatizing songs.

Creates songs during play—often in teasing other children.

*Stories* Delights in the humorous in stories and nonsense rhymes.

Creates stories with silly language and play on words.

*Miscellaneous* High interest in dramatic play.

Great increase in sense of humor.

60 months—*Painting* Begins with idea in mind.

Products usually recognizable.

Pictures usually simple with few details.

Details most important to child drawn largest—often flower larger than house.

Knows colors and uses their names accurately.

Subjects: people, houses, boats, trains, cars, animals, and landscapes with sun.

Often begins to feel inadequate in ability to portray ideas.

*Clay* Recognizable objects generally with purpose in mind—that is, made as gifts or to use in dramatic play in dollhouse, store, etc. Often paints products.

*Blocks* Large groups plan block structure before building, and carry out group enterprise in detail.

Large sturdy structures often combined with other materials, such as boxes, barrels, chairs, etc.

Extensive dramatic play centered around structure, with carry-over of interest for several days.

*Music* Majority can reproduce simple tones accurately from middle C to second F above.

Many can sing short melodies on pitch.

Large repertoire of songs for recognition and appreciation.

Majority can synchronize hand or foot tapping with music.

Majority can skip, hop on one foot, and "dance" rhythmically with music.

*Stories* Spread of interest to function and origin of things.

Beginning of enjoyment of fanciful stories.

Appreciation of aesthetic experiences is established well before artistic expression. By the time the child is 18 months old, he has been responding to music, pictures, and rhymes for many months, but his creative experiences are still very limited, with the exception of rhythmic expression and sound play which may come in the first year of life. His first artistic attempts are simple and random as he experiments with the different media. At 2 years his experimentation is still largely motor and manipulative, but is becoming more vigorous, more defined, and more complicated. He is less individual in his artistic expression than he was earlier, being strongly imitative of his contemporaries. At 3 years, order begins to emerge along with more precision and control in the use of artistic media. Gradually imagination enters (about 4 years) and is combined with humor to form products which are a delight to the child and about which he feels possessive. As he becomes more serious, at 5 years, with a higher level of aspiration which he has difficulty in attaining, he becomes self-conscious concerning his ability and concentrates his talents on more conventional subjects. When his artistic attempts become well organized, the child may lose some of the joys of expression but this joyousness is replaced by a deeper satisfaction in achievement.

Individual differences are perhaps more marked in aesthetic expression than in any other field of behavior. Greatest variation is shown in musical ability. A child of 21 months may sing songs accurately, while some adults never attain this ability. Lack of ability, unless dependent upon physical handicaps, may not show itself during the preschool years, but giftedness in artistic expression may be detected very early.

TABLE 29
OUT-FOR-A-WALK BEHAVIOR

15 months—Walks only a very short distance and then demands carriage.
　　　　　Likes to walk holding on to stroller (rather than on to attendant).
18 months—Runs ahead of adult; interested in all byways.
　　　　　Can often be handled much more easily in a harness.
　　　　　Enjoys the harness. It often helps to break his falls.
21 months—More conscious of adult's presence.
　　　　　Less exploring.
　　　　　May want to hold adult's hand.
　　　　　Enjoys helping to push stroller.
24 months—Lingers over activities along the way—picks up sticks and stones.
　　　　　Adult has to wait, call to child or lure him on to some new interest.
　　　　　Under pressure, child may go in opposite direction.
　　　　　Now may refuse to hold adult's hand except on curbs or walls, which
　　　　　　are a delight.
30 months—Dawdling still persists along the way.
　　　　　May respond to "Good-bye" as adult walks off and leaves; runs to
　　　　　　join her.
　　　　　Holds adult's hand by choice and may not wish to leave adult.
　　　　　Beginning to have thoughts of destination in mind.
36 months—Definitely has thoughts of destination in mind.
　　　　　May refuse to hold adult's hand except at crossings.
42 months—Strong-minded here as in many activities. May refuse to continue
　　　　　　walk. If adult walks away, child remains stock still. May throw
　　　　　　self on ground.
48 months—Runs ahead of adult and waits at the crossing.
　　　　　Resents holding adult's hand to cross street.
　　　　　Wants to go on short errands outside the house. Can manage if on the
　　　　　　same side of the street.
60 months—Can go to kindergarten by himself.
　　　　　Can safely cross streets, if they are not too hazardous, and may even
　　　　　　help a younger child to cross the street.

It will be noted that this chapter, as well as the chapter on language which precedes it, differs from the chapters on motor and adaptive behavior in that it does not deal exclusively with the specific test items listed in our Behavior Schedules. This chapter in particular provides background material as to the development of personal-social behavior in general.

The items that can be scored in the chapters on Behavior Norms and Behavior Schedules which follow (pages 133 to 147) are selected from among the many to be observed in the child's everyday home life. They deal primarily with feeding behavior, toileting, dressing, play, and communication.

A few of the items listed on these Schedules in the Personal-Social category can be observed during the behavior examination. Such behaviors as "Hands cup full of cubes," "Refers to self by pronoun 'me,' " "Repetitive in speech or other activity" can be seen or heard and recorded by the examiner.

Most, however, must be determined in an interview or conversation with the parent or parents. Or, another possible method is to present the parent with a list of interview questions which he or she can respond to and then submit to the examiner.

The personal interview technique is the more desirable as it often elicits supplementary information which would not be covered in a written questionnaire. In a clinical situation we usually arrange for the parent, if needed, to remain in the examining room with the child. The older, or more secure, child will not need this kind of support. In that case our custom is to have the parent, or parents, watch the examination through a one-way vision screen.

After the examination, while the child is being examined by other members of our staff (visual testing, projective testing, etc.), or while he or she is playing in a playroom, the examiner discusses with the parent what the parent has seen of the child's behavior, answers specific questions which the parent may have, and then conducts an interview which will yield answers allowing her to check the Personal-Social items on the Developmental Schedule.

For those who prefer to provide the parent with a list of interview questions, a rather detailed personal-social interview has been prepared (see Appendix C). Data from such an interview were gathered on the present subjects but have not as yet been analyzed. Results will be reported in a subsequent publication (65).

# PART THREE

# 8

## Behavior Norms

| | 2 YEARS* | 2½ YEARS |
|---|---|---|
| **MOTOR** | | |
| Stands: tries, on one foot | | |
| Cubes: tower of 10 | | |
| Drawing: holds crayon by fingers | | |
| **ADAPTIVE** | | |
| Cubes: tower of 8 | | 70% |
| Cubes: aligns 2 or more, makes train | | 75 |
| Drawing: imitates V and H strokes | 32% | 72 |
| Drawing: scribbles in response to circular stroke | | 55 |
| Inc. Man: adds 1 part | | 44 |
| Formboard: inserts 3 blocks on presentation | 37 | (57) |
| Formboard: adapts repeatedly, error | 22 | (48) |
| Color Forms: places 1 | 45 | (68) |
| **LANGUAGE** | | |
| Interview: gives first name | | 64 |
| Interview: tells sex (G) | | 50 |
| Prepositions: 1 to 2 | | 88 |
| Picture Vocab.: 7 correct | | 74 |
| Action Agent: 3 correct | | 53.5 |
| **PERSONAL-SOCIAL** | | |
| Play: pushes toy with good steering | | |
| Play: helps put things away | | |
| Commun.: refers to self by pronoun "me" rather than by name | | |
| Commun.: repetitious in speech and other activity | | |
| Self-help: can put on own coat (not necessarily fasten) | | |
| Temperament: opposite extremes | | |

* All 2-year-old items and those at 2½ in parentheses are from *The First Five Years of Life*, published in 1940.

## 3-YEAR-OLD LEVEL

|  | 2½ YEARS | 3 YEARS |
|---|---|---|
| **MOTOR** | | |
| Walks: on tiptoe, 2 or more steps | | |
| Stands: on one foot, momentary balance | | |
| Skips: tries | | |
| Rides: tricycle, using pedals | | |
| Stairs: alternates feet going up | | |
| Jumps down: lands on feet (G) | | |
| Broad jump: distance 12 inches | | |
| Pellets: 10 into bottle in 26″(G), 24″(B) | | |
| **ADAPTIVE** | | |
| Cubes: tower of 10 | | |
| Cubes: adds chimney to train | 17.5% | 63% |
| Cubes: imitates bridge | 16 | 62 |
| Copy Forms: copies circle | 7 | 83 |
| Copy Forms: imitates cross | 5 | 55.5 |
| Inc. Man: adds 3 parts | 15.5 | 51 |
| Formboard: adapts, no errors or immediate correction of error | (24)* | (59) |
| Color Forms: places 3 | (16) | (57) |
| Pellets: 10 into bottle in 26″(G), 24″(B) | | |
| Counts with correct pointing: 3 objects | 33.5 | 63 |
| **LANGUAGE** | | |
| Interview: gives first and last names | | 85 |
| Speech: uses plurals | | |
| Interview: tells age (G) | 32 | 50 |
| Interview: tells sex (B) | 40 | 78 |
| Prepositions: obeys 3 | 28 | 62 |
| Digits: repeats 3 (1 of 3 trials) | 28.5 | 52 |
| Comp. Quest. A: answers 1 | 37 | 66 |
| Action Agent: 6 to 7 correct | 26 | 67 |
| Picture Vocab.: 11 correct | 40 | 63 |
| **PERSONAL-SOCIAL** | | |
| Feeding: feeds self with little spilling | | |
| Feeding: pours well from pitcher | | |
| Dressing: puts on shoes | | |
| Dressing: unbuttons front and side buttons | | |
| Commun.: asks questions rhetorically | | |
| Commun.: understands taking turns | | |
| Commun.: knows a few rhymes | | |
| Temperament: cooperative | | |

* All figures in parentheses are from *The First Five Years of Life*, published in 1940.

## 3½-YEAR-OLD LEVEL

|  | 3 YEARS | 3½ YEARS |
|---|---|---|
| **MOTOR** | | |
| Stands: on one foot, 2″ or more | | |
| Jumps: both feet leave floor | | |
| Broad jump: distance 19 inches | | |
| Jumps down: lands on feet (B) | | |
| Hops on one foot: succeeds (G) | | |
| Pellets: 10 into bottle in 23″ | | |
| **ADAPTIVE** | | |
| Cubes: builds bridge from model | 35% | 75% |
| Copy Forms: copies cross | 23 | 60 |
| Inc. Man: adds 4 parts | 36 | 49.5 |
| Inc. Man: eyes better than a scribble | 37 | 53 |
| Pellets: 10 into bottle in 23″ | | |
| **LANGUAGE** | | |
| Interview: gives number of siblings | 43 | 62 |
| Prepositions: 4 correct | 45 | 58.5 |
| Digits: repeats 3 (2 of 3 trials) | 44 | 66 |
| Picture Vocab.: 12 correct | 53 | 69 |
| Comp. Quest. A: answers 2 | 37 | 65 |
| Action Agent: 12 correct | 31 | 55 |
| **PERSONAL-SOCIAL** | | |
| Dressing: washes, dries, hands, face | | |
| Play: associative play replaces parallel | | |
| Commun.: calls self "I" | | |
| Commun.: asks "How?" questions | | |
| Toileting: seldom has "accidents" | | |
| Temperament: vulnerable | | |

## 4-YEAR-OLD LEVEL

|  | 3½ YEARS | 4 YEARS |
|---|---|---|
| **MOTOR** | | |
| Stands: on one foot, 2 to 7″ | | |
| Stairs: walks down, foot to a step | | |
| Skips: on one foot | | |
| Jumps: running or standing broad jump | | |
| Broad jump: distance 20 inches | | |
| Beanbag catch: any method | | |
| Pellets: 10 into bottle in 23″ | | |
| **ADAPTIVE** | | |
| Cubes: imitates gate or better (G) | 34% | 57% |
| Copy Forms: imitates square or better | 44.5 | 72 |
| Inc. Man: adds 5 parts | 30 | 65 |
| Inc. Man: arm straight out from body or better | 45 | 60 |
| Pellets: 10 into bottle in 23″ | | |
| **LANGUAGE** | | |
| Identifies some letters | 41 | 61 |
| Identifies some numbers (G) | 46 | 76 |
| Interview: gives age (B) | 43 | 80 |
| Prepositions: 5 correct | 44 | 66 |
| Digits: repeats 3 (3 of 3 trials) | 47 | 54 |
| Digits: repeats 4 (1 of 3 trials) | 38 | 52 |
| Picture Vocab.: 14 correct | 31 | 55 |
| Comp. Quest. B: 1 correct | 36.5 | 61.5 |
| Action Agent: 14 correct | 39 | 70 |
| Counts: 4 objects correctly | | |
| **PERSONAL-SOCIAL** | | |
| Dressing: buttons clothing | | |
| Dressing: washes and dries face and hands, brushes teeth | | |
| Dressing: dresses and undresses, supervised | | |
| Dressing: laces shoes | | |
| Dressing: distinguishes front and back | | |
| Play: cooperates with other children | | |
| Play: builds buildings with blocks | | |
| Develop.: goes on errands outside home (no crossing streets) | | |
| Develop.: tends to go out-of-bounds | | |
| Commun.: asks "Why?" questions | | |
| Temperament: expansive | | |

## 4½-YEAR-OLD LEVEL

|  | 4 YEARS | 4½ YEARS |
|---|---|---|
| **MOTOR** | | |
| Hops on one foot: succeeds (B) | | |
| Broad jump: distance 24 inches | | |
| Beanbag, overhand throw: succeeds (G) | | |
| Beanbag catch: hands vs. chest or better (B) | | |
| Pellets: 10 into bottle in 20″ | | |
| **ADAPTIVE** | | |
| Cubes: makes gate from model | 38% | 64% |
| Copy Forms: copies square recognizably | 35 | 56.5 |
| Copy Forms: divided rectangle—ladder design, side lines straight | 20 | 27* |
| Inc. Man: adds 7 parts | 33.5 | 62 |
| Letters: 1 or 2 recognizable | 35.5 | 72 |
| Numbers: 1 or 2 recognizable | 14.5 | 53.5 |
| Counts: 4 objects, and answers "How many?" | 26.5 | 51.5 |
| Pellets: 10 into bottle in 20″ | | |
| **LANGUAGE** | | |
| Identifies some numbers (B) | 42 | 65 |
| Articulation: not infantile | | |
| Interview: gives names of siblings | 37.5 | 67 |
| Digits: repeats 4 (2 of 3 trials) | 35 | 61 |
| Comp. Quest. A: 3 correct | 40 | 53 |
| Action Agent: 16 correct | 42 | 60.5 |
| **PERSONAL-SOCIAL** | | |
| Commun.: calls attention to own performance | | |
| Commun.: relates fanciful tales | | |
| Commun.: bosses and criticizes | | |
| Play: shows off dramatically | | |
| Temperament: unpredictable | | |

* Never becomes normative. This is the high point.

## 5-YEAR-OLD LEVEL

| | 4½ YEARS | 5 YEARS |
|---|---|---|
| MOTOR | | |
| Stands: on one foot, 9″ or more | | |
| Walks on tiptoe: 5 or more steps | | |
| Skips: using feet alternately | | |
| Broad jump: distance 27 inches | | |
| Pellets: 10 into bottle in 18″ | | |
| ADAPTIVE | | |
| Cubes: 6-cube steps with demonstration | 38% | 63.5% |
| Copy Forms: copies triangle ± | 41 | 54 |
| Copy Forms: divided rectangle—ladder design, side lines slanted | 3 | 22* |
| Copy Forms: all on one page | 46.5 | 65 |
| Inc. Man: adds 8 parts | 41 | 61 |
| Name: prints first name | 47 | 70 |
| Counts: 10 objects correctly | –† | –† |
| Calculates: within 5 | 36.5 | 59 |
| Pellets: 10 into bottle in 18″ | | |
| LANGUAGE | | |
| Picture Vocab.: 15 correct | 43.5 | 75 |
| Comp. Quest. B: 2 correct | 41.5 | 64 |
| Action Agent: 17 correct | 54 | 64 |
| PERSONAL-SOCIAL | | |
| Dressing: dresses and undresses, with little assistance | | |
| Commun.: asks meaning of words | | |
| Play: dresses up in adult clothes | | |
| Play: prints or names a few letters | | |
| Temperament: gentle, friendly | | |

* Never becomes normative. This is the high point.
† Data not available due to uneven recording.

## 5½-YEAR-OLD LEVEL

|  | 5 YEARS | 5½ YEARS |
|---|---|---|
| **MOTOR** | | |
| Stands: on one foot, 12" | | |
| Beanbag, overhand throw: succeeds (B) | | |
| Beanbag catch: hands vs. chest or better (G) | | |
| **ADAPTIVE** | | |
| Cubes: 10-cube steps with or without demonstration (G) | 28% | 50% |
| Copy Forms: copies triangle recognizably | 33 | 51 |
| Copy Forms: divided rectangle—H line crosses V, angled lines may cross V | 30 | 55.5 |
| Copy Forms: diamond, 1 or 2 sides correct | 37.5 | 60 |
| Inc. Man: eyes match in size | 47 | 60 |
| Inc. Man: arm points upward | 48.5 | 61 |
| Counts: 12 objects correctly | –* | –* |
| **LANGUAGE** | | |
| Interview: knows month of birthday | 34.5 | 58 |
| Action Agent: 18 to 19 correct | 49.8 | 74.5 |
| Digits: repeats 4 (3 of 3 trials) | 47.5 | 69.5 |
| **PERSONAL-SOCIAL** | | |
| Money: identifies penny and nickel | | |
| Play: understands games like hide-and-seek and tag | | |
| Temperament: breaking up | | |

* Data not available due to uneven recording.

## 6-YEAR-OLD LEVEL

| | 5½ YEARS | 6 YEARS |
|---|---|---|
| **MOTOR** | | |
| Stands: on each foot alternately | | |
| Broad jump: distance 32 inches | | |
| Beanbag throw: advanced | | |
| Beanbag catch: hands only | | |
| Pellets: 10 into bottle in 16" | | |
| **ADAPTIVE** | | |
| Cubes: 10-cube steps with or without demonstration (B) | 34% | 55% |
| Copy Forms: divided rectangle, 3 lines cross center V line | 31 | 52.5 |
| Copy Forms: diamond, oddly shaped (good shape not till 7 years) | 8.5 | 49 |
| Inc. Man: adds 9 parts | 45 | 71.5 |
| Inc. Man: adds 2 or 3 parts at neck | 38.5 | 62 |
| Adds and subtracts: within 10 (normative at 6½) | 25 | 45 |
| Name: prints first and last (G) (normative at 6½) | 18 | 45 |
| Pellets: 10 into bottle in 16" | | |
| **LANGUAGE** | | |
| Counts: 13+ objects | | |
| Calculates within 10 (6½) | | |
| Interview: knows day and month of birthday (normative at 6½) | 28 | 43.5 |
| Digits: repeats 5 (1 of 3 trials) | 49 | 57 |
| Picture Vocab.: 16 correct | 49.5 | 62 |
| Action Agent: 19 correct | 50 | 71 |
| **PERSONAL-SOCIAL** | | |
| Dressing: ties shoelaces | | |
| Commun.: differentiates A.M. and P.M. | | |
| Commun.: knows right and left (3 out of 3 trials or complete reversal) | | |
| Commun.: recites numbers to 30s | | |
| Temperament: oppositional, emotional | | |

# 9

# BEHAVIOR SCHEDULES

In this version of our testing program, tests are not scored numerically, but use of the Gesell Developmental Schedules, or Behavior Schedules, gives an examiner a quick and clear view of a child's behavior level.

Responses are rated as follows. If the child succeeds at a given item, the examiner marks a + in the right-hand side of the double column of vertical lines preceding the item. If the child fails, the examiner marks a −. If success is questionable, the examiner uses both vertical lines and marks a + −. If the child succeeds at a level above the one indicated at any age, the examiner again uses both vertical lines and marks a + +; she then places a + at the succeeding age.

Thus, say a 2½-year-old is being examined, should he be responding right at age, one would expect mostly plusses for the 2½-year-old items, with possibly a few double plusses and an occasional minus. He might presumably have a few plusses for 3-year-old items as well.

Once all items at the child's key age and at surrounding ages have been checked, an examiner can obtain from the schedules a clear picture of just where the child's behavior rates. As mentioned earlier, since behavior does not always develop all of a piece, it is not unusual to find some fields of behavior substantially ahead of or behind others.

(A more objective scoring of our Gesell Preschool Tests is now in preparation.)

# GESELL DEVELOPMENTAL SCHEDULES

Name      *Age*      *Date*      *Case No.*

KEY AGE   2 ½ YEARS

| 2 YEARS | 2 ½ YEARS | 3 YEARS |
|---|---|---|
| **MOTOR** | | |
| Walks: runs well, no falling | Stands: tries, on one foot | Walks: on tiptoe, 2 or more steps |
| Stairs: walks up and down alone | Cubes: tower of 8 | Stands: on one foot, momentary balance |
| Large ball: (no dem.) kicks | Drawing: holds crayon by fingers | Skips: tries |
| Cubes: tower of 6 to 7 | | Rides tricycle, using pedals |
| Book: turns pages singly | | Stairs: alternates feet going up |
| | | Jumps down: lands on feet (G) |
| | | Broad jump: distance 12 inches |
| | | Pellets: 10 into bottle in 26″ (G), 24″ (B) |
| **ADAPTIVE** | | |
| Cubes: tower of 6 to 7 | Cubes: tower of 8 | Cubes: tower of 10 |
| Drawing: imitates V stroke | Cubes: aligns 2 or more, makes train | Cubes: adds chimney to train |
| Formboard: places blocks on separately (G) | Drawing: imitates V and H strokes | Cubes: imitates bridge |
| Formboard: adapts after 4 trials | Drawing: scribbles to circular stroke | Copy Forms: copies circle |
| Color Forms: does not identify any | Inc. Man: adds 1 part | Copy Forms: imitates cross |
| | Formboard: inserts 3 blocks on presentation | Inc. Man: adds 3 parts |
| | Formboard: adapts repeatedly, error | Formboard: adapts, no errors or immediate correction of error |
| | Color Forms: places 1 | Color Forms: places 3 |
| | | Pellets: 10 into bottle in 26″ (G), 24″ (B) |
| | | Counts with correct pointing: 3 objects |

# KEY AGE

| 2 YEARS | 2½ YEARS | 3 YEARS |
|---|---|---|

## LANGUAGE

| 2 YEARS | 2½ YEARS | 3 YEARS |
|---|---|---|
| Speech: discards jargon | Interview: gives first name | Interview: gives first and last name |
| Speech: 3-word sentence | Interview: tells sex (G) | Speech: uses plurals |
| Speech: uses "I," "me," "you" | Prepositions: obeys 1 to 2 | Interview: tells age (G) |
| Picture Vocab.: 2+ correct | Picture Vocab.: 7 correct | Interview: tells sex (B) |
| | Action Agent: 3 correct | Prepositions: obeys 3 |
| | | Digits: repeats 3 (1 of 3 trials) |
| | | Comp. Quest. A: answers 1 |
| | | Action Agent: 6 to 7 correct |
| | | Picture Vocab.: 11 correct |

## PERSONAL-SOCIAL

| 2 YEARS | 2½ YEARS | 3 YEARS |
|---|---|---|
| Toilet: verbalizes needs fairly consistent | Play: pushes toy with good steering | Feeding: feeds self, little spilling |
| Play: domestic mimicry | Play: helps put things away | Feeding: pours well from pitcher |
| Play: hands cup full of cubes | Commun.: refers to self by pronoun "me" rather than name | Dressing: puts on shoes |
| Play: parallel play predominates | Commun.: repetitious in speech and other activity | Dressing: unbuttons front and side buttons |
| Feeding: inhibits turning spoon | Self-help: can put on own coat (not necessarily fasten) | Commun.: asks questions rhetorically |
| Dressing: pulls on simple garment | Temperament: opposite extremes | Commun.: understands taking turns |
| Commun.: verbalizes immediate experiences | | Commun.: knows a few rhymes |
| Commun.: refers to self by name | | Temperament: cooperative |
| Commun.: comprehends and asks for "another" | | |
| Temperament: gentle, easy | | |

KEY AGE

| 3½ YEARS | 4 YEARS | 4½ YEARS |
|---|---|---|
| **MOTOR** | | |
| Stands: on one foot, 2″ or more | Stands: on one foot, 2 to 7″ | Hops on one foot: succeeds (B) |
| Jumps: both feet leave floor | Stairs: walks down, foot to a step | Broad jump: 24 inches distance |
| Broad jump: distance 19 inches | Skips: on one foot | Beanbag, overhand throw: succeeds (G) |
| Jumps down: lands on feet (B) | Jumps: running or standing broad jump | Beanbag catch: hands vs. chest or better (B) |
| Hops on one foot: succeeds (G) | Broad jump: 20 inches distance | Pellets: 10 into bottle in 20″ |
| Pellets: 10 into bottle in 23″ | Beanbag catch: any method | |
| | Pellets: 10 into bottle in 23″ | |
| **ADAPTIVE** | | |
| Cubes: builds bridge from model | Cubes: imitates gate or better (G) | Cubes: makes gate from model |
| Copy Forms: copies cross | Copy Forms: imitates square or better | Copy Forms: copies square recognizably |
| Inc. Man: adds 4 parts | Inc. Man: adds 5 parts | Copy Forms: divided rectangle—ladder |
| Inc. Man: eyes better than a scribble | Inc. Man: arm straight out from body or | design, side lines straight |
| Pellets: 10 into bottle in 23″ | better | Inc. Man: adds 7 parts |
| | Pellets: 10 into bottle in 23″ | Letters: 1 or 2 recognizable |
| | Counts: 4 objects | Numbers: 1 or 2 recognizable |
| | Identifies some letters | Counts: 4 objects and answers "How |
| | Identifies some numbers (G) | many?" |
| | | Pellets: 10 into bottle in 20″ |
| | | Identifies some numbers (B) |

KEY AGE

| | 3½ YEARS | 4 YEARS | 4½ YEARS |
|---|---|---|---|
| **LANGUAGE** | Interview: gives number of siblings<br>Prepositions: 4 correct<br>Digits: repeats 3 (2 of 3 trials)<br>Picture Vocab.: 12 correct<br>Comp. Quest. A: answers 2<br>Action Agent: 12 correct | Interview: gives own age (B)<br>Prepositions: 5 correct<br>Digits: repeats 3 (3 of 3 trials)<br>Digits: repeats 4 (1 of 3 trials)<br>Picture Vocab.: 14 correct<br>Comp. Quest. B: 1 correct<br>Action Agent: 14 correct | Articulation: not infantile<br>Interview: gives names of siblings<br>Digits: repeats 4 (2 of 3 trials)<br>Comp. Quest. A: 3 correct<br>Action Agent: 16 correct |
| **PERSONAL-SOCIAL** | Dressing: washes, dries, hands, face<br>Play: associative play replaces parallel<br>Commun.: calls self "I"<br>Commun.: asks "How?" questions<br>Toileting: seldom has "accidents"<br>Temperament: vulnerable | Dressing: buttons clothing<br>Dressing: washes and dries face and hands, brushes teeth<br>Dressing: dresses and undresses, supervised<br>Dressing: laces shoes<br>Dressing: distinguishes front and back<br>Play: cooperates with other children<br>Play: builds buildings with blocks<br>Develop.: goes on errands outside home (no crossing streets)<br>Develop.: tends to go out-of-bounds<br>Commun.: asks "Why?" questions<br>Temperament: expansive | Commun.: calls attention to own performance<br>Commun.: relates fanciful stories<br>Commun.: bosses and criticizes<br>Play: shows off dramatically<br>Temperament: unpredictable |

**KEY AGE**

|  | 5 YEARS | 5½ YEARS | 6 YEARS |
|---|---|---|---|
| **MOTOR** | Stands: on one foot, 9" or more<br>Walks on tiptoe: 5 or more steps<br>Skips: using feet alternately<br>Broad jump: 27 inches distance<br>Pellets: 10 into bottle in 18" | Stands: on one foot, 12"<br>Beanbag, overhand throw: succeeds (B)<br>Beanbag catch: hands vs. chest or better (G) | Stands: on each foot alternately<br>Broad jump: distance 32 inches<br>Beanbag throw: advanced<br>Beanbag catch: hands only<br>Pellets: 10 into bottle in 16" |
| **ADAPTIVE** | Cubes: 6-cube steps with demonstration<br>Copy Forms: copies triangle ±<br>Copy Forms: divided rectangle ladder design, side lines slanted<br>Copy Forms: all forms on one page<br>Inc. Man: adds 8 parts<br>Name: prints first name<br>Counts: 10 objects correctly<br>Calculates: within 5<br>Pellets: 10 into bottle in 18" | Cubes: 10-cube steps with or without demonstration (G)<br>Copy Forms: copies triangle recognizably<br>Copy Forms: divided rectangle, H line crosses V; angled lines may cross V<br>Copy Forms: diamond, 1 or 2 sides correct<br>Inc. Man: eyes match in size<br>Inc. Man: arm points upward<br>Counts: 12 objects correctly | Cubes: 10-cube steps with or without demonstration (B)<br>Copy Forms: divided rectangle, 3 lines may angle, cross center V line<br>Copy Forms: diamond, oddly shaped, (good shape not till 7 years)<br>Inc. Man: adds 9 parts<br>Inc. Man: adds 2 or 3 parts at neck<br>Adds and subtracts: within 10 (normative at 6½)<br>Name: prints first and last (G); (normative at 6½)<br>Pellets: 10 into bottle in 16"<br>Counts: 13+<br>Calculates: within 10 (6½ years) |

KEY AGE

| 5 YEARS | 5½ YEARS | 6 YEARS |
|---|---|---|
| **LANGUAGE** | | |
| Picture Vocab.: 15 correct<br>Comp. Quest. B: 2 correct<br>Action Agent: 17 correct | Interview: knows month of birthday<br>Action Agent: 18 to 19 correct<br>Digits: repeats 4 (3 of 3 trials) | Interview: knows day and month of birth-day (normative at 6½)<br>Digits: repeats 5 (1 of 3 trials)<br>Picture Vocab.: 16 correct<br>Action Agent: 19 correct |
| **PERSONAL-SOCIAL** | | |
| Dressing: dresses and undresses, with little assistance<br>Commun.: asks meaning of words<br>Play: dresses up in adult clothes<br>Play: prints or names a few letters<br>Temperament: gentle, friendly | Money: identifies pennies and nickels<br>Play: understands games like hide-and-seek and tag<br>Temperament: breaking up | Dressing: ties shoelaces<br>Commun.: differentiates A.M. and P.M.<br>Commun.: knows right and left (3 of 3 or complete reversal)<br>Commun.: recites numbers to 30s<br>Temperamaent: oppositional, emotional |

# 10

# Examination Techniques

Conducting a developmental examination is quite a different matter from usual testing. With the latter, a score or end product is sought, one which can then be compared with standardized norms. Not that the developmental examination does not deal with end products. But to the developmental examiner, the processes of a child's mind, the ways he behaves, the things he says, are just as important as the final product which can often be misjudged unless we know what steps the child took to reach his goal.

The conduct of the developmental examination in the preschool years requires highly specialized techniques. The examiner must appreciate that there is a gradually increasing awareness of, and ability to adjust to, social situations at this age.

The 2½-year-old has a wholesome restraint with respect to new situations, not being easily led, and following his own devices. The 3-year-old is more open to suggestion and more adaptable; however, his cooperation tends to be sketchy, wayward, and disconnected. The 3½-year-old displays caution and dependency, while the 4-year-old is independent, sociable, talkative, and assertive.

At 4½ years of age, the child is in a stage of fluctuation—at one moment babyish, at another seemingly grown up. The 5-year-old shows a positive form of amenability as well as insight into the subtleties of the testing process. FIVE-AND-A-HALF exhibits strong interest in wanting to become involved, and is ready to ask questions. And then the 6-year-old displays a real eagerness to be examined and a desire to get right to work.

These changes mean not only that the child shows a gradually increasing adequacy in social situations as he grows older, but also that it is necessary to vary the management of the examination to meet the social maturity or immaturity of the child being examined.

## RESPONSES CHARACTERISTIC OF SUCCEEDING AGES

The examiner's approach to the child needs to be extremely cautious at the younger ages and becomes simpler and more direct as the child grows older. Until 4 years of age, children may need to have a parent accompany them during the testing.

### 15 MONTHS

The examiner is very careful not to approach the child directly at this age. During a brief initial interview, questions are addressed to both parents, and then one parent is requested to carry the child to the examining room, even if he is able to walk unassisted.

Because of the strong motor drive at this age, it is best to seat the child in a high chair, rather than at the usual low examining table. The parent makes the placement and then seats herself near the child. If the child protests, he may be allowed to sit on his parent's lap. In either case, test objects are presented on a high table placed in front of the child.

Test materials are presented rapidly, since the examiner understands that demonstration and repeated verbal instructions will not improve the child's performance. Throwing a toy or test object to the floor is the child's way of refusing, so another situation should be offered immediately. Putting the cubes into the cup, once they have been played with, often prevents the child from casting them to the floor.

Except for these special problems of management, the examination procedures used at 18 months of age are also appropriate for children of 15 months.

### 18 AND 24 MONTHS

After parents and child have had some time to explore the waiting area, the examiner enters, closes the door, and, choosing a chair most removed from the child, seats herself at once. A brief conversation is held with the parents, starting with general topics and then moving on to questions in areas that will help the examiner tune in to the child's ability level. (Problems are not discussed.) No direct approach is made to the child at this time, but the examiner needs to be aware of any overtures made by the child and to respond in a pleasant and accepting manner.

Often the child becomes engrossed in books or in a toy he has brought from home. The ideal moment to move to the examining room comes when the child begins to lose interest in his own activity. At this point the examiner looks directly at the child and says, "Let's go play with some toys. Mother is coming, too."

With a nod to the parents, the examiner then leads the way to the examining room. (The parent who does not accompany the child will watch, along with staff members and students, from an observation room equipped with a one-way vision screen.)

Any toy the child has been playing with can usually be removed, with only the offhand comment, "It will wait for us." However, if the child resists, he may bring the toy with him to the examining room where a substitution can be made as soon as he becomes interested in the test materials.

Upon entering the examining room, the examiner states, "This is where the toys are; this is where we play." Closing the door, she points out the parent's chair, the child's chair, and her own, immediately seating herself. If the child clings to his parent, his chair may be moved closer to her, with the comment, "Sit here by Mommy" (or "Daddy"). At the same time, present the large picture book. If real resistance is encountered, the child should be allowed to sit on his parent's lap, and a high table provided for the examination objects.

With the child of this age, the examiner will need to intervene if a mishap such as a broken crayon or a toilet accident occurs, lest the parent chide the child and create unnecessary stress. Prior to testing, a tactful explanation should be given that the parent is expected to lend moral support, but is not to intrude in the examination or to help the child unless requested to do so.

Good balance of the relationship between interest, offer, and surrender is the key to a successful examination at this age. Transitions from one situation to the next must be made with care. Often presenting a new test item will help the child relinquish any materials to which he may be clinging. Verbal instructions should be brief: short, single sentences are best. Always address the child of this age by his name, rather than by personal pronoun. Thus say, "Bobby do it." Dependency on parent and a drive to motor activity are the most common complicating factors here. Phrases such as "All gone," "No more," "Big boy" are often readily accepted and help resolve stressful situations.

## 2½ YEARS

The characteristically oppositional behavior of the 2½-year-old is seen throughout the examination. The techniques used at 2 years of age will still be needed; thus, focus during the initial interview is on the parent, not on the child, and the transition from waiting area to examination room is accomplished with limited verbal instructions.

Once having entered the examining room, the child of this age usually resists direct commands. An indirect approach usually is best in helping him to become involved; it also makes transitions easier from task to task. A parent's presence is still needed, and often helps things to go more smoothly.

The cubes are presented first. If the child does not become immediately involved, the examiner can build a tower of two blocks and then can hand a block to the child, saying, "Put it on top." Often the child will need to rebuild the tower several times before he is ready to try the train. There is quite a bit of exploring of materials at this age, and a hearty "No" response is usually given if the examiner attempts to terminate a situation before the child is ready.

An examiner will find that timing as to when to present things or to finish up a task is very important at this age. Often tasks that are difficult will need to be skipped or presented in parts. Techniques, such as saying, "Look what I have" or "Look what I found," will help direct the child's attention to a new situation.

Many children of 2½ want to keep the test materials. A smooth resolution is to put away finished materials as new ones are presented. When the examination is finished, accompany the child and parent back to the waiting room as if that step, too, were part of the examination.

Motor and verbal objections are customary at this age when any task is too difficult. As will be pointed out in the following chapter, the child may leave the table, throw the material, respond with "No," begin to cry, or just refuse to cooperate. It takes considerable experience and skill to work with a child of this difficult, though delightful, age.

## 3 Years

Things are somewhat easier in the handling of the 3-year-old, but the cautious approach used with younger children is still needed. Without requiring a response, the examiner may now give the child a direct smile and greeting upon meeting. The child should be given time to become somewhat familiar with the examiner and his new surroundings before being taken to the examining room. But as soon as his interest in his surroundings begins to lag, the examiner can start the transition from the waiting area to the examining room.

If the child seems fully at ease, the examiner may offer her hand and say, "Shall we go play with some toys?" The child may or may not accept the hand, but if he accepts the verbal invitation, the examiner tries gently to separate the child from the parent by saying, "Mother (or Daddy) will wait," and to the parent, "We'll be back soon." She then starts for the door, keeping up a patter about where the toys are.

If the child is hesitant about going alone, the examiner quickly shifts and says, "Mother (or Daddy) can come too." Separation of child from parent should never be forced, and in cases where the child starts out bravely but then has second thoughts, the examiner should always be ready to say, "Let's get Mother (or Daddy) too." This holds true even if the child's need for his parent does not make itself apparent until the middle of the examination.

Many children of this age walk into the examining room and seat themselves spontaneously. If the child is uncertain as to what is expected of him, the examiner may say, "That's your chair and this is my chair. Let's look at the blocks." If the child does not seat himself but stands in position behind the table, the fact that he is not seated is ignored and the examiner begins testing. As at the younger ages, as soon as he becomes really interested, the child will usually seat himself spontaneously. It is seldom necessary to enlist the mother's help at this age, even if it has been necessary for her to accompany the child into the examining room. However, if her help is needed, the examiner should not hesitate to call her.

There are usually few refusals at this age, but when they do occur, the examiner may say, "We'll do it later." When a task is represented, if the child still refuses, this second refusal should be accepted. One can often bargain with a 3-year-old by saying, "Let's do this now and then we can . . ." (offering something that hopefully will appeal to the child).

### 3½ YEARS

This tends to be a difficult age to examine. The child of 3½, perhaps because he is uncertain, anxious, and very insecure, seems to feel a strong need to control any situation. However, he may be very cooperative in the examination situation. Certainly he does best if the examiner is fully aware of his inadequacies and sensitivities.

With the 3½-year-old, one needs to be well aware of things that may go wrong or have started to go wrong—and to guard against them (or quickly to shift and cover up once they have gone wrong). The child of this age can often be reached through the parent (if she has needed to accompany him to the examining room). It may help to have her sit very close to him and participate in the examination on cue. In fact at this age it is not unusual to begin the examination by having the parent present the tasks while the examiner retreats to a distance that is less threatening to the child than if she were close.

Many children of 3½ resist the language tasks when they are first introduced, requiring the examiner to change the usual order of the examination. And even once into the examination, the 3½-year-old's responses are mixed with demands that "You do it," "Don't look," or "Look at me"—or "Don't talk" or "Talk."

Hand tremor is often seen during block building. Also some children stutter and others exhibit rapid ticlike eye movements. Verbal refusals are now the leading type of refusal with "I can't" being added to the earlier "I don't know" or "No."

### 4 YEARS

The examiner's initial approach to the 4-year-old can be more direct than with the younger child, though it should still be cautious. After a brief visit in the reception area, the examiner may say, "I have some toys to show you. Let's go see them. Your parents will wait for us here." And to the parents, "We'll be back soon."

Most children will go with the examiner unquestioningly if she seems to expect it, and though they may inquire about their parents during the examination, most are readily reassured when told that they are waiting. If any real problem is encountered in separating the child from his parents, one parent should still be invited to accompany the child, though now as a passive onlooker.

Many children of this age are apt to run ahead of the examiner. Upon reaching the examination room, FOUR often chooses the big chair, but will shift to the child's chair upon suggestion.

As at earlier ages, the examination must proceed fairly rapidly. Transitions, as a rule, are accomplished without difficulty. Many 4-year-olds will ask to go to the toilet in the course of the examination. Both verbal and physical overflow are now seen, with much wiggling, standing up, foot shuffling, as well as asking questions and telling stories and even making personal remarks about the examiner: "My, you have big feet!" Most tasks are completed rapidly without much concern for detail.

The examiner needs to maintain a fast pace and not linger too long on any one task. At the same time it helps to let the child talk while tasks are being shifted and at occasional relief points. The child's inability to perform a difficult task is covered up by him at this age by such comments as "Mommy doesn't want me to do that." FOUR's enthusiasm tends to make him a delight to examine, but an examiner must remember not to press too hard, or to try too hard to hold the child in line.

## 4½ YEARS

Behavior fluctuates between what might be expected at 4 and at 5 years of age. Sometimes the out-of-bounds 4-year-old behavior predominates and then, at the next moment, the focalness and effectiveness of 5. This is an age of uncertainty, inconsistency, and unpredictability—an in-between time when the child's earlier age and his upcoming one are both in evidence but are not as yet well integrated.

At 4½ the transition from the waiting area to the examination room is usually made quite easily. During the examination, the child of this age exhibits a short attention span as he did at 4, but now he is less likely to ask, "Can I go now?" Written work is still completed rapidly, and there is a strong tendency to improvise; that is, the child starts out to make one thing and it changes to something else in midstream.

Limits may need to be set when the child begins to exhibit his earlier out-of-bounds 4-year-old ways. And in examining a child of this age, the examiner should not be surprised if the child's behavior changes to the point where it does not seem to be the same child at the end of the examination as at the beginning. Be alert and ready for surprises!

## 5 YEARS

The 5-year-old child sees the examination as a series of tasks imposed on him by an adult who stands in somewhat of a teacher role. He now is able when placed in the examination situation to take his cues from the adult; that is, he adapts more than he did earlier. The examiner as a result may need to adapt less than formerly.

The child now can be greeted openly and directly by the examiner, and will quickly move with her to the examination room after an explanation of the reason for his visit.

Most children at 5 are quite able to separate from their parents with ease. They may question as to their parents' whereabouts during the examination, but rarely insist on seeing them. In fact the presence of a parent in the examining room is not only unnecessary but is also less desirable than formerly, since at 5 the child is more self-conscious than he was at a younger age.

FIVE as a rule willingly accepts the examiner's hand, and he holds her hand as they move toward the examining room. Once there, the child goes directly to the chair allotted to him and sits quietly, awaiting instructions.

The child of this age wants to cooperate and to do well. Thus he will ask orienting questions such as, "Where should I put it?" or "How long should I make it?" Such questions should be answered with a permissive, "Any place" or "As big as you like." There is less general conversation at this age than at 4 and at 4½, when the child may have kept up a running commentary as he worked.

An almost adultlike pencil grasp is now seen. The child's paper is not shifted as yet, and he often moves his nondominant hand across the page as he works. Very little motor overflow occurs at this age. When under tension, a child may lift his buttocks slightly from his chair or may bend from the waist. But as a rule he does not leave his chair as he often did at earlier ages.

The child of 5, though basically focal and not talkative, is easily distracted by sights and sounds, and may comment about them without actually interrupting his work. If he does not know the answer to a question, he may excuse himself with, "My mommy never told me." Or he may say, "My mommy told me" or "My teacher teached me" when asked how he knows something.

Since the child of this age is extremely vulnerable, the examiner needs to show great sensitivity and to maintain an easy, noncritical give-and-take approach. She must know how and when to shift her approach and when to give up. It is more important to maintain rapport and to make the child feel that he is doing well than to complete every test or to attain a special response on any one test.

## 5½ YEARS

The child of this age is less focal and less concerned with pleasing than he was at 5. However, the transition from the waiting room to the examining room is usually accomplished easily. The child may take the examiner's hand when it is offered, but if he does so he then quickly drops it, wishing to be on his own. Body movements as he walks are not as compact as earlier. Arms swing wide rather than being held close to the body. Once in the examining room, the child easily slips into his chair and is ready to start to work.

While working, the child's nondominant hand is usually placed flat on his paper, with the little finger separated from the rest of the fingers, rather than all fingers being held tightly together as they were at 5. The pencil may be held in an almost adultlike grasp.

At this age the child often loses visual orientation, consequently he may make many letter and number reversals. His eyes sweep over the room rather than consistently focusing on the task at hand, but there are few orientation questions and less need than earlier for examiner approval. At times the child may sit with a finger in each side of his mouth. Often there is a running commentary about what is going on: "That's easy!" Or the child tries to get out of a tight situation with, "I forgot" or "I can't."

In general the child at 5½ needs only minimal instructions in order to carry out the required tasks, since it is easy for him to adapt to the examination situation.

## 6 YEARS

The 6-year-old is eager to be examined and ready for this new experience. He comes to the examining room readily and seats himself quickly. Once seated, he buckles right down to work. He works so rapidly that he may even drop his pencil in his haste. In fact, the examiner may find it difficult to keep up with the 6-year-old, not only as he moves from the waiting room to the examining room but also during the testing itself.

Body posture now shifts to the nondominant side. The nondominant hand is usually placed flat on the paper, with all the fingers spread apart. As the child of this age writes, he often presses so hard that he breaks his pencil point. Sometimes his writing goes uphill.

At this age, sudden insights are experienced with an explosive "Oh!" which tells the examiner that the child has come to a full understanding of a task. Reversals may be recognized and corrected, even though erasures tend to be sloppy. Throughout an examination the 6-year-old frequently asks, "What?"—a clue that because of excessive speed he has heard only part of a direction given.

The child of 6 does not like to repeat things, and will characteristically complain, "I already did that" if a new activity is similar to something previously required. He often talks aloud as he works, demonstrating his need for auditory reinforcement of his activity. Comments such as "That's easy" and "I forgot" are often heard.

Nothing makes a 6-year-old happier, however, than solid praise for his efforts.

TABLE 30
SUGGESTED ORDER FOR PRESENTING TEST SITUATIONS

Cubes
Name, Numbers
Copy Forms
Incomplete Man
Language Questions
Discriminates Prepositions
Digit Repetition
Picture Vocabulary
Comprehension Questions
Action Agent
Counting Pennies
Pellets into Bottle
Gross Motor

Color Forms and the Three-Hole Formboard (at appropriate ages) are interspersed wherever the examiner feels they will be appropriate in relation to each child's response to the total situation. Often they fit well between Comprehension Questions and Action Agent.

# 11

## Overflow, Refusal, and Variant Behavior Characteristic of Succeeding Ages

Many years of research and clinical work have led us to the conclusion that almost everything the young child does or says reveals not only his individuality but his behavior level as well. Thus even when he is not cooperative in responding to our test situations, his very way of refusing tells a good deal that one needs to know about him. That is, not only do test responses change in a patterned, predictable way but also the child's way of refusing the tests (7).

Even when a child does cooperate with the examiner, he or she often expresses some behaviors not addressed strictly to the task at hand. These overflow behaviors, as well as actual refusals, embellish our picture of the child's response and help establish the age level of his behavior. Refusals and other variant or overflow behavior can thus be considered not apart from or detracting from more positive responses, but rather as an integral and significant part of the entire response.

With the very young child, the 18-monther and the 2-year-old, the chief way of refusing a test is some kind of motor refusal, most often leaving the examining table. The second most common way is some form of emotional refusal, chiefly crying or clinging to mother.

However, even by 30 months, verbal refusals equal in number mere motor refusals and exceed emotional refusals; and by 3 years of age and following, the predominant kind of refusal or variant behavior is verbal.

Figure 3 illustrates the extent to which each of the more common kinds of variant behavior—motor, verbal, emotional, reverted, and

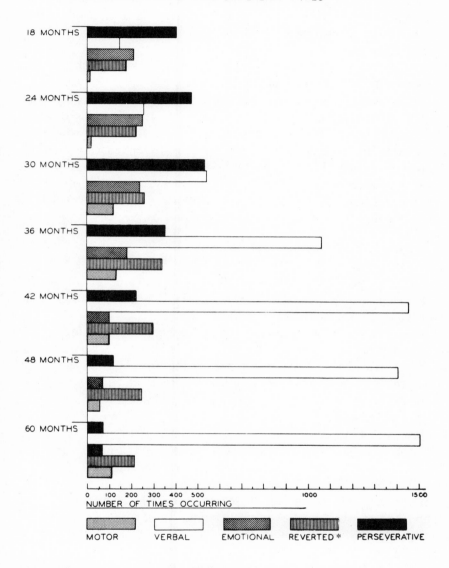

VARIANT  BEHAVIOR   (18 to 60  months)
AGE  DISTRIBUTION  OF  FIVE  DIFFERENT  TYPES

* Reverted behavior is appropriate behavior, but at a lower age level.

FIGURE 3  Age Distribution of Different Kinds of Variant Behavior, from 18 months to 5 years

perseverative—occurred in a group of 50 subjects each at 18, 24, 30, 36, 42, 48, and 60 months. Motor, verbal, and emotional behavior speak for themselves. Reverted behavior is a kind of response which occurs when a child stays with the test situation (for instance, Cubes or Copy Forms) but behaves in a manner characteristic of a younger child. In perseverative behavior the child simply goes on and on with some single response.

This chapter describes some of the more common ways in which children at succeeding ages behave during the behavior examination. However, it must be remembered that each child grows at his own rate and in his own way. Even when the sequences we describe hold true, each child has his or her own individual *timetable*. Also some children seem out-of-bounds at every age; while others are quiet and contained. Thus the descriptions of age levels which follow should be taken only as guidelines, not as gospel.

## 2½ YEARS OF AGE

The 2½-year-old, at home or abroad, tends to be a difficult little person. We have described him as living at the "opposite extreme" of whatever the adult wants him to do.

Thus in the examination situation he needs to be handled with considerable skill. Special techniques are required. A very confident though friendly attitude on the part of the examiner is needed. It is helpful if he or she can be casual, as if expecting that of course the child will go along with suggestions. It is important to avoid questions which can be answered with "No," such as "Would you like to play with some toys?"

Move fast and talk fast. Be prepared to ignore a failure or refusal and to move on quickly to something more appealing.

At 2½, as Figure 3 shows, the child is apt to express refusal in a motor way—throwing objects, leaving the table. But this is also the first age at which verbal refusals equal motor ones. Thus the child may say "No" or "Don't know" or (seeking an ally) "Mummy do it."

Some emotional refusals still persist. The child may possibly cry or cling to his mother or even need to sit in her lap during the examination.

This is not always an easy age at which to obtain a full examination from a child. But if the examiner will keep in mind that even refusals tell their story and provide clues to developmental level, an examination, even though difficult, can be extremely revealing. It is also a challenge to the examiner.

## 3 YEARS OF AGE*

The 3-year-old, by nature a rather docile and cooperative individual, is much easier to examine than the child just younger. THREE likes people and he wants to please them. He likes to cooperate. In some ways he is an ideal candidate for an examination.

Also his increased proficiency, particularly his expanding vocabulary and greater control of language, seem to make it much easier for him to cope with the examination situation. Particularly does his language interest stand him in good stead. Fatigue or lack of interest can often be countered with, "Now let's do it a *different* way."

However, some refusal or inability is still met with and, in the case of a difficult or not too cooperative child, an examiner will do well to preface her directions with; "How about doing so-and-so?" rather than giving a direct command.

The total examination, however, is rendered much easier than previously by the fact that even when the child does not wish to comply, refusals and objections tend to be couched in verbal rather than in motor or emotional terms. The child can say, "I don't know" or "I don't want to" in a gentle way when some one thing is too hard, without disrupting the general flow of the examination.

And one can often bargain with THREE; thus, an examiner may say, "As soon as we do this, we'll do . . ." something else which will appeal to him.

By 3½, motor ways of refusing—leaving the table, banging things on the table, or throwing things—have now sunk to third place as a type of noncooperation. Reverted behavior, staying with the situation but reverting to a more immature way of behaving, that is, making a train or tower with the cubes when asked to make a bridge, now places second.

If one is aware of and makes allowances for uncertainties and insecurities, as a rule the examination goes reasonably well at this age.

* This and material which follows in this chapter is adapted from Frances L. Ilg, Louise Bates Ames, Clyde Gillespie, and Jacqueline Haines, *School Readiness* (New York: Harper & Row, 1978).

## 4 YEARS OF AGE

The 4-year-old, in the examination as elsewhere, tends to be somewhat out of bounds. As we have often remarked, FOUR is wild and wonderful. But he tends to be out of bounds in every field of behavior. Motorwise, it is hard for him to sit still; he is very active. His language definitely tends to be out of bounds. Even in the examination, bathroom language is apt to come in, and the Incomplete Man often has a belly button.

His exuberant emotions, too, make themselves evident during the examination. He enjoys it so much. But when he tires of it, he makes it all too clear that he would like to leave: "Can I go back now?" or "When are we going to be through?"

As he approaches the examining room, he is likely to run on ahead. He may not want to sit at the table, but once seated, he may not be able to inhibit himself from picking up the pencil and starting at once, even before the examiner has had a chance to give directions.

His Copy Forms products tend to be expansive; he may need more than one sheet of paper. And throughout the examination, he talks and talks, telling the examiner a great deal about himself and his family and friends. He is apt to ask quite personal questions of the examiner: "Do you sleep here?" "Do you have any children?" Refusals are now almost entirely verbal.

His enthusiasm makes him, as a rule, a pleasure to examine, but a successful, experienced examiner will anticipate and appreciate his out-of-bounds tendencies and will not be overzealous about holding him in line.


## 5 YEARS OF AGE

This is a pulled-in, focal age of good adjustment. FIVE lives close to home and wants to be good and to please others. He seems all put together. There is a surety to his movements. Gone are his far-flung, out-of-bounds 4-year-old ways.

FIVE likes to obey and to do what he is told. He is by nature cooperative, and in an examination he likes to follow what he thinks are the rules, to do what the examiner asks of him, to please the examiner.

The child of this age seems compact and taut posturally and, as he walks, his arms tend to be held close to his body. Though he re-

sponds briefly when directly asked a question, he is not the bub-
bling-over talker that he was a year earlier.

FIVE keeps his body and paper straight, picks up his pencil directly and does not transfer it from hand to hand. He moves up close to
his work and there is relatively little overflow. The pencil tends to
be held in a three-fingered grasp, near its tip, with the shaft
oblique.

There is marked restraint throughout. FIVE sometimes holds himself rather stiffly in his effort to be "good" and to do what is expected of him. He may occasionally bounce a little in his chair, but
seldom stands or asks to finish or to leave the table. His docility and
wish to please tend to make him an easy person to examine, though
one senses his vulnerability. As just earlier, refusals if any are almost entirely verbal.

## 5½ YEARS OF AGE

Behavior at 5½ tends to be very different from what it was six
months earlier. At home, parents note that the child now tends to
explode, to oppose, to demand, to strike out, even to strike against.
It is as if behavior were loosening up and expanding.

We are not surprised, then, that in the examination the child of
this age is somewhat different from the focal, concerned, trying-to-
please person he was at 5. Now he is more ready to speak up, to
question if he does not understand, to carry out commands with
only minimal instruction.

He is also less anxious to please and to do things exactly right.
He feels more confidence in himself than he did, and is more ready
for give-and-take. The examiner is less conscious of needing to pro-
tect him. His body now moves with a looseness, having lost the
stiffer erectness so characteristic of 5.

Paper as a rule is still straight on the table top, and if there must
be an adjustment, the child shifts his head and not the paper.

Eyes are less steadily focused on the task at hand. They may
sweep boldly over things in the examining room. Overflow is seen in
the fact that, though the body continues active, as earlier, most total bodily activity is confined to wiggling in the chair or banging
knees together. The child seldom actually leaves his seat at the examining table.

As at all ages, there are some verbal digressions, some comment
that things are hard, or that the child does not know or cannot do

something requested. Much overflow at this age is in the mouth region. The child's tongue extends and sweeps over his lips, participating fully in the act of writing, and clearly showing points of increased strain.

At this age and at the age which follows, we get relatively few refusals. Overflow behavior seems to represent merely physical ways of expressing extra energy, rather than being a motor expression of refusal of tasks, as at the earlier ages.


## 6 YEARS OF AGE

At 6 the behavior first seen half a year earlier achieves full expression. The 6-year-old is extremely expansive, enthusiastic, eager. He takes part in an examination happily, not so much from a wish to please as from eagerness for any new venture. In fact, whatever he does, he does with impulsive enthusiasm. His exuberance is contagious.

The child of this age is much concerned with balance, possibly because of his own balance problems. He does not sit quietly, but is likely to balance on the back two legs of his chair. He may even try to balance on only one, and fall to the floor. Or he may kneel in his chair. Sitting still is very difficult at this age.

As he works, his head is likely to be tilted to the nondominant side, and he may tilt his paper at an angle. The spread of arms, noted as he walks, may also be observed as he sits at the table with arms outspread. He rotates his paper with his nondominant hand.

Eyes sweep out laterally and his tongue may still be very active in moving over both upper and lower lips. Or he may try to inhibit this by pushing his tongue against his lower lip or the inside of his mouth.

Fingers are frequently brought to the mouth. The child also chews on his pencil or on any loose tabs of clothing material. Throat clearing can be almost ticlike.

The total body is very active, as the child moves in his chair or falls out of it. There are many hand-to-mouth gestures: bringing little finger to mouth, chewing on pencil, picking at teeth, or rotating hands outward in a characteristically expressive gesture.

A typical 6-year-old boasts a great deal—"That's easy"—especially when things are actually difficult for him. And he is a glutton for praise. It is hard to praise him too much.

# PART FOUR

# 12

## Sex and Group Differences

### SEX DIFFERENCES

In spite of much popular and even semiscientific literature, as well as an entire political movement which appears to maintain that all or most sex differences in behavior are the result of our treatment of children and our expectations, present data confirm the position of genetically oriented investigators.

It has been our own observation over the past 50 or so years that substantial, inborn differences do exist between the behavior of girls and that of boys. And it seems to us that these differences are not caused primarily by anything that adults do or do not expect or require.

True, society as a whole may expect boys to be "boyish" and girls to be "girlish," and these expectations do to some extent influence behavior. However, those with experience in the scientific observation and testing of young children are fully aware that, in general and with certain exceptions, girls develop more rapidly than do boys and are thus more advanced in measurable kinds of behavior.

It is not realistic to assume that parental expectation alone is enough to cause girls to walk earlier than boys, talk earlier, be toilet trained earlier. Nor is it realistic to assume that parental expectation causes girls to copy a square, triangle, and divided rectangle earlier than boys do; to add more parts to the Incomplete Man form; to respond to Interview Questions earlier; to repeat digits sooner and more accurately; to count sooner; to print letters, numbers, and name sooner.

The ordinary parent presumably may not even be aware that girls do most of these things earlier than do boys. Parents may indeed pressure their girls to be docile and gentle; their boys to be strong and bold. But it is not realistic to assume that they encourage their daughters to add more parts to the Incomplete Man form than do their sons.

It is our opinion, then, that it is the earlier maturation of girls compared to boys rather than anything that parents (or society) expect or require that causes the marked differences in behavior of the two sexes which we customarily observe.

Present data confirm our observation that in general girls in our culture attain most measurable abilities somewhat sooner than do boys. Table 31 illustrates the fact that with minor exceptions, so far as the tests in question are concerned, girls do reach the various stages of development about six months sooner than do boys.

TABLE 31
SEX DIFFERENCES IN RESPONSE TO
GESELL DEVELOPMENTAL TESTS

|  | GIRLS | BOYS |
|---|---|---|
| CUBES: | | |
| Tower of 10, 3 years | 95% | 67% |
| Train with chimney, 3 years | 60 | 65 |
| Imitates bridge or better, 3 years | 58 | 66 |
| Bridge from model, 3½ years | 82 | 88 |
| Imitates gate or better, 4 years | 50 | 36 |
| Six-cube steps (with dem.), 4½ years | 40 | 36 |
| Ten-cube steps (with or without dem.) | 5½ years | 6 years |
| COPY FORMS: | | |
| Imitates V and H strokes, 2½ years | 80% | 65% |
| Circular scribble in imitating circle | 50 | 60 |
| Copies square, 4½ years | 61 | 48 |
| Copies triangle ±, 4½ years | 47 | 35 |
| Divided rectangle, H or other line crosses center, 5½ years | 60 | 51 |
| INCOMPLETE MAN: | | |
| Adds 1 part, 2½ years | 50% | 38% |
| Adds 3 parts, 3 years | 50 | 52 |
| Adds 4 parts, 3½ years | 62 | 37 |
| Adds 5 parts, 4 years | 70 | 60 |
| Adds 7 parts, 4½ years | 66 | 56 |
| Adds 8 parts, 5 years | 77 | 45 |
| Adds 9 parts, 6 years | 77 | 66 |
| Arms straight out from body, 4 years | 62 | 57 |

|  | GIRLS | BOYS |
|---|---|---|
| Arms meet body line | 4½ years | 5 years |
| Eyes match in V placement | 4 years | 4½ years |
| Eyes match in size, 5 years | 62% | 47% |
| Leg of good length | 5 years | 5½ years |
| Adds 2 to 3 parts at neck, 6 years | 37 | 37 |

INTERVIEW:

| | | |
|---|---|---|
| Gives own age | 3 years | 4 years |
| Gives sex | 2½ years | 3 years |
| Gives number of siblings at 3 years | 57% | 40% |
| Gives number of siblings at 3½ years | 70 | 55 |
| Knows month of birthday | | |
| At 5 years | 45 | 24 |
| At 5½ years | 60 | 26 |
| Knows day and month of birthday | | |
| At 5 years | 32 | 5 |
| At 6 years | 42 | 45 |

MOTOR TESTS:

| | | |
|---|---|---|
| Hops on one foot | 3½ years | 4 years |
| Jumps down, lands on both feet | 3 years | 3½ years |
| Throws beanbag overhand | 4½ years | 5½ years |
| Beanbag catch, hands vs. chest or better | 5½ years | 4½ years |

PREPOSITIONS:

| | | |
|---|---|---|
| Obeys 1 to 2, 2½ years | 84% | 92% |
| Obeys 3, 3 years | 65 | 59 |
| Obeys 4, 3 years | 52 | 38 |
| Obeys 5, 4 years | 86 | 47 |

DIGITS:

| | | |
|---|---|---|
| Repeats 3 (1 of 3 trials) | | |
| 2½ years | 36% | 21% |
| 3 years | 46 | 58 |
| Repeats 3 (2 of 3 trials) | | |
| 3½ years | 72 | 66 |
| Repeats 3 (3 of 3 trials) | | |
| 4 years | 60 | 48 |
| Repeats 4 (1 of 3 trials) | | |
| 4 years | 60 | 44 |
| 4½ years | 77 | 68 |
| Repeats 4 (2 of 3 trials) | | |
| 4 years | 50 | 20 |
| 4½ years | 65 | 57 |
| Repeats 4 (3 of 3 trials) | | |
| 5½ years | 75 | 64 |

|                                                          | GIRLS | BOYS |
|----------------------------------------------------------|-------|------|
| Repeats 5 (1 of 3 trials)                                |       |      |
|    5½ years                               | *54*  | 44   |
|    6 years                                | 54    | *60* |
| COUNTS:                                                  |       |      |
|   With correct pointing, 3 objects, 2½ years   | *45%* | 22%  |
|   Counts to 4 and answers "How many?"          | *71*  | 32   |
| PRINTS:                                                  |       |      |
|   Prints 1 or 2 letters                        |       |      |
|    4 years                                | *50%* | 21%  |
|    4½ years                               | *86*  | 59   |
|   Prints 1 or 2 numbers                        |       |      |
|    4½ years                               | *78*  | 29   |
|   Prints first name                            |       |      |
|    4½ years                               | *56*  | 38   |
|    5 years                                | *88*  | 53   |

To supplement present data, we include information from an earlier study made on older children, which supports current findings as to the general behavior advancement of girls over boys. Subjects whose behavior was chosen as a basis for this comparison were examined in the schools of North Haven, Connecticut. The mean IQ of these subjects as tested on the WISC was 105. Forty % of parents fell chiefly in Class III of the Minnesota Scale of Parental Occupations.

Observed differences were as follows (45):

## PENCIL AND PAPER TESTS

### Writing Name

Girls lead in writing letters of consistent size at every age. Differences in making an even base line are inconsistent, but from 7 years on favor girls. Girls lead in correct use of capital letters up till 7 years of age, after which all children respond correctly. Girls make fewer reversals than do boys at 5½ years of age. Cursive writing becomes normative for both at 8 years.

Girls tend to write slightly smaller and thus are considered advanced in this respect. Girls do somewhat better at writing their first name at 5 years, the two sexes performing equally well thereafter. They do better than boys at writing their last name at 5 and 5½ years; performance is even thereafter.

Thus, with minor exceptions, any differences in success of writing name are in favor of girls.

### Writing Address

Girls are a little ahead of boys in successful writing of number, street, city, and state, and success on all of these becomes normative in girls at 8 years, in boys at 9. A marked difference does appear at 9 years when 92% of girls, only 64% of boys, write their whole address without error. Here, again, differences throughout the age range are small, but definitely favor girls.

### Writing Numbers

Girls are slightly ahead of boys in number of figures made (5 and 5½ years). Girls space numbers evenly before boys do: over 50% of girls space evenly by 8 years of age; boys do not reach this effectiveness till 9. Girls are also slightly ahead of boys as to evenness of figures in that 68% of girls, only 50% of boys, make even figures at 7 years, when such performance is first normative. Girls are also somewhat ahead in using front of paper only for their figures.

Again, differences are small, but in almost every instance they favor the girls.

## COPY FORMS

### Circle

Differences here are fairly marked. Girls are considerably ahead of boys. Sixty-six % of girls start the circle at the top at 5 years, 82% by 5½. Starting at the top does not become normative in boys till 5½ years (56%), and at every age through 8, more girls than boys start it at the top.

Also, more girls than boys use a CCW direction through 8 years. Girls predominantly use a CCW direction even at 5 years (58%). This direction is not normative in boys till 5½ years (58%).

### Cross

More girls than boys at both 5 and 5½ years draw V-line downward, H-line from L to R. Girls achieve a qualitatively "good" cross at 8 years, boys not until 9.

### Square

In general more girls than boys draw the square CCW and start with the left side down. More boys draw CW, and their place of starting is much more varied.

### Triangle

More girls than boys use one line at 5, 5½, and 6 years; more boys than girls use one line only from 8 to 10 years. More boys than girls use three lines (presumably a less mature pattern) at 5, 6, and 7 years. However, all of these trends are highly variable.

At most ages more girls than boys start with left side down. Performance of boys is slightly more variable than that of girls. However, at most ages boys make more continuous CCW lines than do girls, and at every age through 8 years more girls than boys make immature or younger patterns.

### Rectangle with Diagonals

So far as the outer part of this product (the rectangular shape) is concerned, performance of girls is ahead of boys at 5 years in that more girls than boys make a continuous single line. A continuous single CCW line occurs equally (44% of each) in girls and boys at 5½ years, but in more girls than boys at 6 years (56% girls, 44% boys). Thereafter trends are varied. In general girls seem to be slightly ahead of boys through 6 years; and boys slightly ahead of girls thereafter, but these trends are not clear-cut.

So far as the inside pattern of the rectangle with diagonals is concerned, the performance of boys is slightly ahead of girls through 5½ years, in that younger patterns drop out a little sooner in boys. Thereafter girls seem somewhat more advanced than do boys though differences are slight and inconsistent.

### Diamond—Horizontal Orientation

Younger patterns occur to a slightly larger extent in girls than in boys through 7 years of age. Horizontal or vertical split pattern, which appears to be the most mature response, occurs more in boys than in girls at 5½ and 6 years, but more in girls than in boys at 7 to 10 years. Drawing in a continuous single direction occurs more in boys than in girls throughout.

### Diamond—Vertical Orientation

Sex differences are slight and somewhat inconsistent. Drawing one or more lines in a continuous direction comes in somewhat sooner in boys than in girls. At the older ages a vertical or horizontal split pattern (the most mature pattern made) shows up a little more strongly in girls.

### Three-Dimensional Forms

Girls are ahead so far as copying the cylinder is concerned, from 5 to 7 years of age. Boys are ahead from 8 to 10 years.

Boys, however, are slightly ahead throughout on copying the cube face-on, and definitely ahead throughout in copying the cube point-on.

### Organization of Copy Forms on Page

Girls are ahead of boys at every age so far as number of forms which are of an even size; and even size becomes normative in girls at 9 years, not quite normative in boys (46%) even by 10 years. Girls are also ahead in that horizontal placement of forms on the paper becomes normative in girls at 7 years; in boys, not until 10 years.

As to placing forms in an orderly horizontal direction, girls are ahead of boys at 5, 7, 8, and 9 years. Orderly horizontal direction becomes normative in girls at 7 years; in boys, not until 10 years.

## INCOMPLETE MAN

Girls add more parts than boys do, on the average, from 5 to 8 years of age. Girls are also ahead of boys in achieving good length of leg, in adding a pupil to the eye, in completing the neck area, and in giving facial expression.

Boys are ahead of girls in placement and direction of arm, in making good fingers, and in placing the ear correctly. Other sex differences are small and variable.

This perhaps overabundance of evidence on sex differences is included here in an effort to convince parents and teachers that "real" differences do exist in the behavior of the two sexes. As will be seen, many if not all of these differences are of a kind which could hardly have been caused (as some claim to be the case) by parental expectation.

## GROUP DIFFERENCES

A second and similar question often asked is whether children today are better informed and/or quicker and smarter or relatively more mature at any given age than were children several decades ago.

In the present instance we are comparing 2- to 6-year-old boys and girls examined by us in the 1970s with 2- to 6-year-olds we examined in the 1930s. The world has changed markedly in the past 40 years. Have the children?

The two groups of compared children are rather similar from a socio-economic point of view. Most are white, middle-class boys and girls of a New England background. As indicated before, they were selected on a slightly different basis: earlier subjects were chosen from a somewhat narrower band of parental occupations. Their parents, classified according to Florence Goodenough's Occupational Categories, were 90% from Groups III and IV (Group I being her highest occupational category, and Group VI the lowest). One hundred percent of parents fell in categories III, IV, and V. The parents of present subjects represented, in the proportion in which they appear in the U.S. Census figures for 1960, 11 categories from professional down through laborer.

However, though selected somewhat differently, basically each group was representative more or less of a middle-class population.

Table 32 indicates an almost remarkable similarity between the responses of the two groups. In 30 out of 51 comparisons made, that is, in 59% or just over half the measures, *scored behavior occurred at exactly the same time* in each of the two groups of children.

## TABLE 32

## PRESENT NORMS COMPARED WITH 1940 NORMS

| | 1940 Norms | Current Subjects |
|---|---|---|
| **2½ Years** | | |
| Cubes: builds tower of 8 | * | * |
| Cubes: aligns 2 or more, train | At 2 years | * |
| Cubes: adds chimney to train | ** | At 3 years |
| Drawing: imitates V and H strokes | * | * |
| Interview: gives full name | * | First name only |
| Picture Vocab.: 7 correct | * | * |
| **3 Years** | | |
| Cubes: tower of 10 | * | * |
| Cubes: imitates bridge | * | * |
| Drawing: copies circle | * | * |
| Drawing: imitates cross | * | * |
| Digits: repeats 3 (1 of 3 trials) | * | * |
| Action Agent: 7 correct | * | * |
| Interview: tells sex | | |
| Girls | * | At 2½ years |
| Boys | * | * |
| Comprehension in Quest. A: answers 1 | * | * |
| Obeys prep. ball and chair | Two commands | Three commands |
| Picture Vocab.: 11 correct | * | * |
| **3½ Years** | | |
| Cubes: bridge from model | * | * |
| Digits: repeats 3 (2 of 3 trials) | * | * |
| Comp. Quest. A: answers 2 | * | * |
| Picture Vocab.: 12 correct | * | * |
| Action Agent: 9 correct | * | 12 correct |
| Prepositions: obeys 3 | * | Obeys 4 |
| **4 Years** | | |
| Cubes: imitates gate | * | * |
| Drawing: copies cross | * | At 3½ years |
| Inc. Man: adds 3 parts | * | Adds 4 parts |
| Counts with correct pointing: | | |
| 3 objects | * | At 3 years |
| Action Agent: 13 correct | * | 14 correct |
| Obeys 4 prepositions | * | At 3½ years |
| Picture Vocab.: 14 correct | * | * |
| Pellets into bottle: 10 in 25″ | * | At 3 years |

*A star in one column means that the behavior occurs at the age in question. A star in both columns means that the two sets of norms agree.

** An interpolated figure, not actually arrived at.

|  | 1940 NORMS | CURRENT SUBJECTS |
|---|:---:|:---:|
| **4½ YEARS** | | |
| Cubes: gate from model | * | * |
| Drawing: copies square | * | * |
| Counts: 4 objects | * | * |
| Digits: repeats 4 (1 of 3 trials) | * | (2 of 3 trials) |
| Action Agent: 14 correct | * | 16 correct |
| Comp. Quest. B: 1 correct | * | At 4 years |
| **5 YEARS** | | |
| Cubes: builds 2 steps | * | * |
| Inc. Man: adds 7 parts | * | Adds 8 parts |
| Action Agent: 15 correct | * | 17 correct |
| Comp. Quest. B: 2 correct | * | * |
| Picture Vocab.: 15 correct | * | * |
| **5½ YEARS** | | |
| Drawing: copies triangle | * | * |
| Drawing: copies rectangle with diagonals | * | * |
| **6 YEARS** | | |
| Cubes: builds 3 steps | | |
|    Girls | * | At 5½ years |
|    Boys | * | * |
| Drawing: copies diamond | *† | *† |
| Inc. Man: adds 9 parts | * | * |
| Digits: repeats 4 (2 of 3 trials) | * | Repeats 5 |
|  | | (1 of 3 trials) |
| Picture Vocab.: 16 correct | * | * |
| Calculates: within 5 | * | At 5 years |

*† Product resembles diamond but not a "good" copy of diamond in either group.

For fewer than half of the measurable comparisons were there differences between the two groups. In 18 of the 21 instances, present subjects were approximately six months ahead of earlier subjects. Present treatment of data did not check as to the statistical reliability of these differences, but the consistency of the direction of the differences suggests that in certain respects children today are slightly advanced developmentally compared to children of the 1930s.

Causes of these differences are not certain but can be surmised. Children today are exposed to cultural influences, such as television programs, for instance, aimed specifically at advancing behavior. Parents today are bombarded with books which advise them on how to advance their children's behavior. And possibly more effective,

just as improved diet has resulted in a generation of children physically taller on the average than their parents and grandparents, the
same improved diet may conceivably have resulted in physically
more effective and advanced behavior.

# 13

## Practical Uses of the Gesell
## Behavior Tests

The practical uses of our Gesell Preschool Tests have over the years turned out to be many and varied. Before we list and describe them, however, it may be useful to explain again what it is that a behavior or developmental examination reveals. Also it is important to make as clear as possible the difference between the Developmental Quotient (DQ) and the Intelligence Quotient (IQ).

A Behavior or Developmental Examination tells us how far a child's body has come, in action. It reveals the approximate age (based on standard norms) that his behavior has reached. Thus it tells whether any given boy or girl is behaving in a manner which matches, falls below, or runs ahead of his chronological age.

There has been some confusion over the years as to the relationship between the so-called DQ (Developmental Quotient) and the IQ (Intelligence Quotient). These two measures are in some instances quite different and yet they are often confused.

The Intelligence Quotient as commonly defined relates rather strongly to the child's purely intellectual abilities, and many of the best-known intelligence tests relate clearly to the child's verbal or cognitive abilities. An attempt to broaden these tests so that they will include something more than verbal ability is found in the WISC (Wechsler Intelligence Scale for Children) which has two parts—Verbal and Performance.

In general, though, IQ is measured chiefly in relation to the individual's verbal ability. The Gesell Behavior or Developmental Tests, in contrast, measure four fields of behavior: motor, adaptive, language, and personal-social.

In infancy, though a majority of the behaviors measured are motor, there appears to be a reasonably close relationship between DQ and IQ. Other things being equal, a 9-month-old infant who, on the totality of our tests, rates at or above 9 months is in all likelihood of at least average if not above-average intelligence.

That is, there appears to be a reasonably good relationship between the two measures. In fact, a study of our own (2) has shown that even through the first ten years of life, early behavior tests actually do correlate rather well with later tests of so-called intelligence.

Admittedly not everyone agrees with these findings. And in spite of this evidence, we must admit that in many individual instances there can be a marked discrepancy between the two measures.

Thus a child with a high IQ might be young for his age in general behavior ways. This discrepancy is of special importance when it comes to entering children in school. Thus a child with even an exceptionally high IQ may in his total behavior not be ready for the grade to which his chronological age or the law in his community assign him.

In short, though the two measures—DQ and IQ—may run fairly close in infancy, as the child matures it is quite possible for them to be rather far apart.


## A. TO DETERMINE DIFFERENCE BETWEEN IMMATURITY AND RETARDATION:

The difference between immaturity and retardation is one of the more difficult things to explain clearly. Let's say a 24-month-old child responds, on the Gesell Behavior Tests, at an 18-month level (that is, he is six months behind the norm). Should we call him retarded or merely immature?

The determination, since it is made chiefly on the basis of clinical experience, is difficult to explain objectively. If, to the examiner, the child appears to be (body and behavior) within quite normal limits, but simply behind the norm for his age, we call the behavior immature. That is, we assume basic normality and simply a benign slowness in development.

If the child seems dull, and the total appearance of both body and behavior give the impression that intelligence as well as behavior level is substantially below his age, then we tend to label the behavior retarded or defective.

We appreciate that this explanation will not be particularly satisfactory to all readers or users of our tests. We can merely say that extensive clinical experience tends to give an examiner a good clinical "feel" for the difference.

## B. THE BEHAVIOR EXAMINATION AS A NEUROLOGICAL EXAMINATION:

Our position, and one which Dr. Gesell initially emphasized, is that behavior is a function of structure—that as our bodies are built, so they behave. This is particularly true of behavior as it changes with age. In the absence of a complete neurological examination, it has seemed to us that if an infant's or child's behavior is up to what is expected of an individual of his age, it is reasonably safe to assume that his nervous system is intact.

We feel confident in saying that the infant who at 40 to 44 weeks can poke a pellet or other tiny object with his forefinger or can get to his hands and knees and creep, or the child who at 4 years of age can copy a square from a model and who has no major deviations of sight or hearing is in all likelihood neurologically sound.

This particular use of our behavior examination is of special use to parent or pediatrician in those cases where seeming slowness of behavior may have caused parental concern.

## C. USE BY PARENTS SEEKING GENERAL ORIENTATION:

However, there are many parents today who, even though reasonably secure about their child's normality, nevertheless find themselves wanting to know what it is reasonable to expect of their boy or girl at any given preschool age. This interest is felt not necessarily in the spirit of competition, but rather as a matter of orientation.

Simple, clear-cut, and realistic norms can be of use to a parent in these days when so many are being bombarded with books which tell them "How to Raise a Superior Child," "How to Teach Your Baby to Read," "How to Increase Your Child's Intelligence." Some have been led by the specialists to believe that any child who is not reading and writing numbers by 3 years of age may be in some way deficient.

Many parents do find norms such as presented in this book useful in assuring them that their child, even though not reading or reciting numbers before kindergarten entrance, may be fully normal for his age.

In short, many quite noncompetitive parents still find a simple road map of the stages through which their child's behavior will develop to be of interest.

## D. USE IN CASES OF ADOPTION:

One special value of behavior tests is in cases of adoption (though because of changing times they have not been used in recent years as fully as they might have been).

Back in the 1940s many responsible social agencies, in supervising the placement of infants and young children in adoptive homes, took special pains to determine that each adoption candidate was behaviorally as well as physically sound.

Their special concern was to avoid placing infants and children who gave every evidence of being retarded in families to whom this retardation would be an obvious surprise and disappointment. Though this notion of "matching" babies to families, that is, of placing potentially normal children in families which could give them advantages, was ignored or even ridiculed by some social agencies, it seemed important to many.

Then society changed. Many agencies believed that it would be the adoptive parents' handling that would determine how the children ultimately turned out. Others encouraged the placement of so-called "hard to place" children. (These included the physically or mentally handicapped, older children, children from minority groups.) Thus developmental examining in many instances fell into disuse.

Now the placement of, for instance, black children in white families is being vigorously discouraged by the Black Social Workers' Association.

Also the relative shortage of adoption candidates is resulting in many families being willing to accept any available infant or child.

In spite of all these changes, we still recommend strongly a careful behavior as well as a physical examination of any adoption candidate. The more a family knows about the endowment and potentials of a new member, the better prepared they are to do a good job of parenting.

### E. USEFULNESS IN DETERMINING SCHOOL READINESS:

A final and extremely important use of behavior tests is one that we have been emphasizing for the past two or more decades. This is its use in determining that boys and girls are correctly placed in school.

This is a use not even considered in the 1940s. We were at that time fully aware of the fact that no child can or should be expected to perform in a way that exceeds his behavior stage regardless of his chronological age. Our tests were used to help parent, pediatrician, psychologist to appreciate what could and could not be expected of any given child in the way of accomplishment.

Yet strangely enough we did not initially apply this principle and point of view to the child in school. We went along with those many others who assumed that some certain chronological age (usually 5 for kindergarten, 6 for first grade) automatically made a child ready for school. Exception was made by some for those children who were extremely bright or who were early readers. It was not unusual for a 6- or even 5-year-old who could read at second-grade level to be placed in second grade.

Both of these concepts—that a certain birthday age and/or advanced reading ability made a child ready for school—have been given up slowly.

But gradually we ourselves—and only more gradually parents and educators in general—have come to appreciate and accept the notion that it is behavior age and not birthday age, IQ, or reading ability which should best determine the time of school entrance.

Our current position is that perhaps 50% of school failures could be prevented or cured by proper placement based on a child's behavior age. Much of our time and effort in the past 20 years has been devoted to researching this notion. Such research is presented in our book *School Readiness* (43) which has been recently revised.

This point of view has been tried out, sometimes under our direction, sometimes independently, in school systems throughout this country and abroad. The following examples of cities or towns which have successfully used developmental placement should suffice:

Thus unpublished research from Visalia, California, has shown that by using developmental placement *a school can sharply reduce the number of children who need remedial help*. In one primary school of 500 children, before use of developmental placement, there were 58 referrals outside the school for special help in one year. The next year, with developmental placement, only 8 children had to be referred outside the school for special help.

In Garden Grove, California, at the Genevieve M. Crosby School, the 1966–67 first-graders served as a control group, while all kindergarten children the next year were placed developmentally. There were sharp contrasts in the performance of the two groups. Sixty-five % of the control group read below grade level, whereas only 8% of the developmentally placed children read below grade level.

A report from the developmental examiner in the Gwinette County, Georgia, elementary schools indicates that

> For the educator, grasping the developmental point of view could be the beginning of a new way of life. In September 1971 approximately 1,800 Scott Foresman Reading Readiness tests were given to incoming first graders. On the basis of this test, it was determined that *only three out of ten* children would most likely be successful in a first-grade reading program and would read on a first-grade level. It also seemed that Fall birthday children, and boys more than girls, would have trouble.
>
> This led to the realization that maturity was a major factor that had not been taken into account. Many of the children were in trouble not because they were slow, not because they had not had adequate preschool experience, but because they needed time to grow.
>
> Thus the school provided not only a readiness class for all who needed it, but also gave all children readiness tests before their placement was determined.
>
> Using age (6 years) as a criterion for first-grade entrance, the Scott Foresman survey showed that only 54% would be ready for reading. Using developmental age as a criterion, 71% would be ready to read. There was a greater predictive rate between behavior readiness and reading success than between chronological age and reading success.

In the 1940s and 1950s the Gesell Behavior Tests were taught mostly to and used mostly by psychologists and pediatricians. At present they are being taught to and used by educators as well. Our own methods of instruction in the giving of behavior examinations are offered largely through one-day seminars, one-week introductory workshops, and one-week advanced workshops. These workshops are given by Gesell Institute staff under the direction of Programs for Education*, and are held either at the Gesell Institute in New Haven or in local communities throughout the country.

An early warning of immature behavior which might indicate needed delay in beginning kindergarten or first grade may be noted as early as 3 years of age. Parents or educators who are concerned about maturity often request, or use, a behavior test at 4, 4½, or 5 years of age. Many school systems now routinely provide what they call prekindergarten screening, using our own or other behavior tests to examine all children who on the basis of their chronological age would be ready to begin kindergarten.

It is our hope and expectation that this present volume will be helpful to those teachers, psychologists, guidance personnel, administrators, and parents who are concerned with the use of the developmental examination as the basis of correct grade placement.

When such an examination is not available, birthday age alone can offer a clue, although it is not as accurate as a behavior age evaluation. But it is safe to say that if a child is on the older side when he starts school, it will stand him in good stead.

Regardless of state or local custom, we prefer that a girl be fully 5 years old before she begins kindergarten; 6 for first grade. We like boys to be 5½ for kindergarten; 6½ for first grade.

Of all the possible uses of the Gesell Behavior battery, its use in relation to determining the most favorable time for starting school or for subsequent promotion of students may turn out to be one of its most substantial contributions.


### F. ASSESSMENT AS OPPOSED TO TESTING:

It has been of concern to some over the years that, although our Gesell Behavior Tests do reveal the approximate age level of any child's behavior, they do not provide a specific numerical score.

In this respect we quote from a statement in a book titled *Psychological and Educational Assessment of Minority Children* (56), edited by Thomas Oakland. He writes in the introduction to this volume, "It is important to distinguish between testing and assess-

---

* Programs for Education, Inc., 1200 Broadway, New York, N.Y. 10001. Telephone number: (212) 689-3911. Or contact Gesell Institute, 310 Prospect Street, New Haven, Conn. 06511.

ment. Testing is to be done with assessment in mind, but assessment does not necessarily result in a score. The functions of assessment are classification and educational programming, decision making and intervention. The limitations of decision making based on test scores should be kept in mind, for testing is not equivalent to assessment, and assessment is not an end in itself."

# 14

## Further Ways of Measuring and Describing Behavior

This book, aside from giving a general description of the behavior to expect at each of the first six years, has dealt almost exclusively with behavior testing. Its chief purpose has been to present our Gesell Preschool Tests and to explain how to give, score, and use them.

However, it seems fair to parents and professionals alike to mention at least briefly that there are numerous other valuable kinds of tests which we use ourselves or through referral to other specialists.

### INTELLIGENCE TESTS

Among the most maligned and at the same time most useful of such tests are the so-called intelligence tests. From 6 years and up, we use the WISC (Wechsler Intelligence Test for Children [66]), both the verbal and the performance scales. Below six, we use the Slosson Intelligence Tests (62). We agree with those who insist that no one should consider an IQ score as gospel. But we do not agree with those who consider such tests either unnecessary or unfair.

Nowadays all too many children of such low intelligence that they belong in special classes for the retarded are shunted into so-called "Learning Disability" classes, without anyone facing or perhaps even knowing that these children are simply lacking in intelligence.

Some insist that intelligence testing is discriminatory. Our opinion is that there is discrimination *against* a child if school and family do not know that he or she is substantially below average in intelligence (when this is the case) and needs to be treated accordingly.

## PROJECTIVE TECHNIQUES

A second kind of test or technique, equally as important as the intelligence test, is the group known as Projective Techniques. Such tests are those to which there is no right or wrong response. Rather, they consist of neutral situations onto which the subject projects various aspects of his personality or individuality. We consistently use such tests.

The one which seems to us the most effective is the well-known Rorschach Inkblot Test. Our personal contributions regarding this test (16, 17, 18) suggest or substantiate the position that, even in a rather free-flowing test of this sort, age or developmental changes, as well as personality factors, show themselves clearly. It has been our experience that the Rorschach offers a veritable X ray picture of the subject's psyche.

In fact we consider that the child's response to the standard ten Rorschach inkblots reveals developmental age, general intellectual level, stability or instability of personality, adequacy and accuracy of perception, as well as special aspects of individuality.

And, though it has never achieved the acceptance which we had wished, we also use the Lowenfeld Mosaic Test (6) routinely. This test consists of a box of different colored poker chips of various shapes—square, diamond, and equilateral, right-angled isosceles, and scalene triangles. The subject is given a 10¼ by 12⅜-inch piece of white paper and is asked to "make something" with the chips.

Responses reveal, supposedly, not only the age level of performance but also something about basic individuality. Dr. Margaret Lowenfeld, the originator of this test, suggested that the Rorschach tells us how the individual experiences, but the Mosaic tells how he functions.

A third projective test which in clinical practice we have found to be extremely revealing is the Kinetic Family Drawing Test (KFD) of Burns and Kaufman (22, 23). In using this test the examiner merely suggests to the subject that he or she draw a picture of "Everybody in your family doing something." Children react to this instruction with remarkable alacrity, and the depths of personal and family feelings revealed are often truly amazing.

One further similar test which has been proposed but not as yet described in book form is the Color Tree Test. This is very simply given. The subject is presented with a box of colored pencils and a sheet of paper and is asked to draw a tree. As with other projective techniques, if properly evaluated, this test reveals both developmental level and individuality. A manual describing this test is currently in preparation.

## EVALUATION OF VISUAL BEHAVIOR*

For the sighted child, learning and establishing perceptual experiences occur mainly through use of vision. From the moment of birth, the child begins to build a visual construct of the world about him. As he matures, he will be able to utilize his vision to discern relationships in his environment that can be stored as experiences. These learned visual experiences may later be recalled to evaluate new objects or situations.

Should a child be visually impaired, his development may be delayed, depending upon his ability to adapt to his impairment and compensate for his visual loss by utilizing other senses with which to learn. A child, however, does not necessarily have to be visually impaired to have vision interfere with his learning process and his general development. Vision can interfere with learning and development because of many more subtle difficulties.

Over the past 25 or more years, we have found that a thorough evaluation of the child's vision is a necessary and useful complement to the Gesell Preschool Behavior Tests. For this reason, the staff at the Gesell Institute has always included optometrists specially trained in the field of children's developmental vision.

Just as preschool development can be monitored by developmental tests, visual development can also be monitored. We have found that delays in development as measured by Gesell developmental tests are often accompanied by or caused by visual difficulties. These difficulties may manifest themselves as abnormal developmental refractive changes such as myopia (nearsightedness), hyperopia (farsightedness), astigmatism, or as problems in the binocular function of the eyes. These manifestations in turn can affect or interfere with the child's perceptions of his visual world. As an end re-

*This section has been contributed by Dr. William Padula, Director of Visual Research at the Gesell Institute.

sult, the learning process may be affected, thereby slowing the development of the child.

Only through a knowledgeable understanding of child and visual development can these interferences be detected and dealt with correctly.

At the Gesell Institute visual examinations include testing in several areas. The examination begins with the Keystone Screener Instrument. During this portion of the evaluation, the examiner observes the child's adjustment to the testing situation as well as screening his visual and perceptual abilities.

The second portion of the evaluation examines Visual Performance Skills. In this section the examiner analyzes the way the child utilizes his vision under specific testing situations, such as the ability to track a moving object; where the child postures accommodation (focusing mechanism) and convergence (where his eyes are pointed) when he looks at a near object; depth perception; visual acuity at distance and near; and the readability range.

A thorough eye health examination is also performed, including an external and internal evaluation. An in-depth history concerning health, disposition, and learning styles is taken. Such aspects of health as allergies, nutritional deficiencies, and endocrine metabolism are probed and related to the visual examination.

A complete refraction is performed. The purpose of this part of the examination is to determine the developmental refractive status of the child. Information about how the child visually relates to various positions in space and how the child is adapting to the stresses in his life are determined.

Additional visual and motor perceptual tests are also administered. These include tests for eye, hand, and foot preference; balance; coordination; spatial perception; figure-ground; transformations; motor-equivalence; perceptual constancy; representation; and so on.

Although the visual examination produces specific findings that are related to the developmental abilities of the child, the examiner includes as part of the evaluation an observation of the child's behavior during all portions of the preschool testing. By combining the results of the findings with the aspects of observed behavior and history, the examiner is then able to derive a more complete view of the child's abilities and inabilities.

No other form of examination has proved a more useful supplement to the Gesell Preschool Behavior Tests than a careful examination of the child's vision. Performed by qualified professionals, a visual examination can be given to a child of any age, including early infancy. We recommend that every child receive a visual examination during the first year of life and every year thereafter until the age of 5. Because of the rapid changes that occur in visual development and because of the importance of warding off visual interference for normal development, we strongly recommend biannual visual examinations for children between the ages of 5 and 12.

## SIDEDNESS

Laterality, or sidedness, and especially handedness, has always been of considerable interest to those concerned with human behavior. Fortunately, long gone are the days when some Freudians considered that only obstinate, poorly adjusted people who hated their mothers would even think of using their left hands. Long gone too are the times when people forced naturally left-handed children to use their right hands.

There is still division of opinion as to whether or not mixed dominance is harmful. Some consider that it is best for people to use right eye, right hand, right foot—or left eye, left hand, left foot (28). Others consider that mixed dominance is not necessarily harmful, even though confused dominance obviously may be.

At any rate handedness and general sidedness have long been topics of interest. But it is only recently that the public has become especially interested in the fact that presumably left-brained individuals behave in a different manner from right-brained individuals. It is generally accepted that the left cerebral hemisphere governs language functions and verbal communication and the time sense, whereas the right cerebral hemisphere governs visual-spatial configurations and manipulatory performance. Left-brained individuals tend to be good at reading, talking, describing, whereas right-brained individuals may be better at performing. Left-brained individuals may be best oriented in time; right-brained persons, in space. It is also generally considered that left-brained individuals tend to be right-handed; right-brained individuals, left-handed.

California educator Madeline Hunter (40) suggests that many of our schools teach more toward the left-brained child than to the right. She points out that schools for the most part have been beaming most of their instruction through a left-brained input (reading and listening) and output (talking and writing), thereby handicapping children not skilled in these special areas.

At any rate, the child's sidedness and especially the degree of unilaterality are things that we wish to observe. Certainly some children, though clearly right-handed, quite easily use their left as a helping hand. Others are so completely right-handed that they do not even use their left hand to steady their paper as they write. In general, function does seem more effective if a nondominant hand, or eye, can at least play its part.

## THE CHILD'S NUTRITIONAL STATE

One aspect of child behavior which has long been of major interest to us is behavior as influenced by the child's physical status. In past years it was necessary for us to refer our clinical subjects to outside sources for this kind of evaluation. From now on hopefully much of this kind of evaluation can be accomplished at our own institute under the supervision of our new director, Sidney M. Baker, M.D., a generalist with special interest in orthomolecular medicine, nutrition, allergies.

Among the aspects of physiological response influencing behavior which has interested us especially is the effect of an allergic reaction on the child's behavior. According to Dr. Ray Wunderlich (67):

> It works both ways. Allergy can interfere with the function of the brain and the brain that doesn't work properly can bring on allergy. There is a growing realization that the adjustment problems of children are more often biologically based than was commonly recognized in the past. The ability of tranquilizers, anticonvulsants, stimulants, vitamins, and minerals to alter brain function leads us to look for further explanation of behavior within the child, at the cellular and subcellular levels.

Thus as he points out, the child who falls asleep over his desk after lunch may not be so much one who has not had enough sleep the night before as the one who is experiencing an allergic reaction to something he ate at lunch. The child who seems hyperactive, irritable, tense, may be reacting to something as specific as the toner in a copy machine or some solution used by the janitor in cleaning the classroom.

Wunderlich assures us that

A child with hyperactivity, poor attention span, distractability, and aggressiveness may become completely normal when an offending food is removed from his diet. Or the direct use of medication as corticosteroid drug treatment can within a few days improve his behavior abruptly. Attention span may lengthen, sleep disturbances may go away, aggression and violence diminish.

One of the best-known proponents of the important notion that the food we eat may strongly influence our behavior is Dr. Ben Feingold (29). In his much publicized book *Why Your Child Is Hyperactive,* he stresses that a poor diet, especially the ingestion of artificial colorings and flavorings, can have a very bad effect on behavior. He believes that improper diet is a specific cause of hyperactivity and learning difficulties.

A more recent book along the same lines is Dr. Lendon Smith's *Improving Your Child's Behavior Chemistry* (63). Dr. Smith asks "Why do so many children turn out so badly, in school and in life?" He thinks it is because their bodies just do not work right. Some bodies work in such a way that their owner's brains do not get the proper nourishment.

If the cortex, or forebrain, is not properly nourished, the animal or emotional brain takes over. With nothing to stop him, the child often becomes violent and aggressive. Thus he sees a match and nothing in his brain acts to tell him *not* to burn down the schoolhouse.

As Smith explains it, the proper functioning of the forebrain depends on constant nourishment, since it cannot store up nourishment. Improper diet, especially the consumption of too much white flour and sugar, can interfere with the body's functioning. Too much sugar, for instance, lowers the blood sugar in the body to the extent that the forebrain does not function. The Dr. Jekyll/Mr. Hyde child who is so good one minute and dreadful the next may actually be suffering from a malnourished forebrain due to improper diet.

In short, there are many different and useful ways of assessing a given child's endowment, of determining his strong points and his weak ones. No one has a copyright on the very "best" test or kind of measurement. Whatever battery one uses, there may always be some gaps. But the amount of testing that even the most ardent clinician can do is finite. Time is finite. Money to pay for testing is finite. Parental and child patience are finite.

The best one can attempt is a reasonably circumscribed group of tests which will answer the critical question at the moment. In assessing any individual child's developmental status, which in our experience is basic in determining what either school or family can expect of him, during the past half century we have found that our Gesell Developmental Examination offers a true and useful picture of where any given child is functioning and thus of what it is fair for his environment to expect of him.

# Appendix A:
# Materials*

*Materials and recording sheets may be purchased from Programs for Education Book Service, Box 85A, Lumberville, Pennsylvania 18933. Or contact Gesell Institute, 310 Prospect Street, New Haven, Conn. 06511.

## MATERIALS*

*Action Agent:*
Card listing the following 20 questions:

| | |
|---|---|
| 1. What scratches? | 11. What sails? |
| 2. What sleeps? | 12. What boils? |
| 3. What flies? | 13. What floats? |
| 4. What bites? | 14. What growls? |
| 5. What swims? | 15. What stings? |
| 6. What burns? | 16. What gallops? |
| 7. What cuts? | 17. What aches? |
| 8. What blows? | 18. What explodes? |
| 9. What shoots? | 19. What roars? |
| 10. What melts? | 20. What mews? |

*Ball:*
Large white rubber ball with red and green stripes encircling the middle. Diameter 6 cm. (SR 4526, Seamless Rubber Company, New Haven, Connecticut 06511.)

*Beanbag:*
A rectangular bag 4½ inches by 2½ inches. Made of corduroy (narrow welt), filled with beans or little stones. In solid color: red, green, or blue.

*Color Forms:*
Five red forms pasted on a white card 8.5 by 11 inches. Circle: 5 cm. in diameter (upper right); square: 5 cm. (upper left); triangle: 6.5 cm. (lower left); semicircle: 8 cm. in diameter (lower right); Maltese cross: 7 cm. in length and 2.5 cm. in width of arms (center). Five red cardboard shapes of corresponding size and shape.

*Comprehension Questions:*
Sheet of paper listing three questions for Group A and two for Group B as follows:

GROUP A:
"What must you do when you are hungry?"
"What must you do when you are sleepy?"
"What must you do when you are cold?"

GROUP B:
"What must you do when you have lost something?"
"What must you do before you cross the street?"

*Most or all of these materials have already been described under the appropriate tests, but for the convenience of the reader are listed here again. This list includes materials used by the child. Examiner's recording sheets are illustrated on pages 200 to 207, Appendix B.

*Copy Forms:*
White cards 8 by 5 inches with following forms outlined in black in center of each card: circle: diameter 8 cm.; cross: lines at right angles, 7.5 cm.; square: 7 cm.; triangle: equilateral, 9.5 cm.; divided rectangle: rectangle 10 by 6.5 cm. with crossed lines inside it, one vertical from top to bottom and one horizontal from side to side plus two angled lines from left top corner to bottom right corner, and from top right corner to bottom left corner, crossing V and H lines at their intersection; diamond: (horizontal) 5.5 cm. each side, top angle 125°; (vertical) same diamond presented vertically.

*Cubes:*
An 8½-by-11-inch sheet of green paper and ten red one-inch square cubes.

*Incomplete Man:*
Blue letter-size sheet of paper with printed form of Incomplete Man and a sharp No. 2½ lead pencil.

*Pellets and Bottle:*
Ten pellets 8 mm. in diameter, flat on one side and convex on the other. A glass bottle 7 cm. in height and 2 cm. in diameter at the opening.

*Pennies:*
Twenty pennies.

*Performance Box:*
Open-ended rectangular wooden box, 16″ by 10″ by 7½″, painted green.

*Picture Vocabulary:*
Eighteen cards in a ringed booklet showing pictures of: airplane, telephone, hat, ball, tree, key, horse, knife, jacket, boat, umbrella, foot, flag, cane, arm, jackknife, pitcher, leaf.

*Three-Hole Formboard:*
A formboard half-inch thick and 36 by 16 cm. in size, dark green in color. Three holes are cut equidistant from each other and from the edges of the board from left to right as follows: circle, diameter 8.7 cm.; equilateral triangle, 9.3 cm.; square, 7.5 cm. Three white wooden forms to fit the holes, each 2 cm. thick: circle, diameter 8.5 cm.; equilateral triangle, 9 cm.; square, 7.3 cm.

# Appendix B:
# Examiner's Recording Sheets*

*Recording sheets and materials for testing may be purchased from Programs for Education Book Service, Box 85A, Lumberville, Pennsylvania 18933. Or contact Gesell Institute, 310 Prospect Street, New Haven, Conn. 06511.

## Face Sheet

Name_____

Age_____

**Final thumb-nail summary of behavior**

**Recommended group**

**Total impression and summary**

**Teachers comments**

# Cube Tests—Recording Sheet

Name_____
Age_____

**Spontaneous**

**Tower**

**Train**

**Bridge**

**Gate**

**Steps (6)**

**Steps (10)**

**Interview Questions, Pencil and Paper,**
**Incomplete Man—Recording Sheet**

Name_____

Age_____

**Interview Questions**

What is your name?_____

When is your birthday?_____

How old are you?_____

Do you have brothers and sisters?_____

Are you a boy or a girl?_____

How many (names, age 3)?_____

**Pencil and Paper**

Copy Forms R_____ L_____

Pencil Grasp_____

**Incomplete Man**

What does this look like to you?_____

**When completed ask:**

Now how does he look?_____

If no answer—say you finish him then you can tell.

Record parts as completed vertically. _____

How does he feel inside?_____

Is he happy or sad?_____

How can you tell?_____

## Prepositions, Digits, and Picture Vocabulary—Recording Sheet

Name_____

Age_____

**Discriminates Prepositions**

(Hand the child a small cube)

Now put the block *on* the chair

Now put the block *under* the chair

Now put the block *in back* of the chair

Now put the block *in front* of the chair

Now put the block *beside* the chair

**Digit Repetition**

Directions (I'm going to say some numbers and when I am through I want you to say them. Listen carefully.)

| | | |
|---|---|---|
| 6 4 1 | 3 5 2 | 8 3 7 |
| 4 7 2 9 | 3 8 5 2 | 7 2 6 1 |
| 2 1 8 5 9 | 4 8 3 7 2 | 9 6 1 8 3 |
| 2 9 4 8 1 6 | 9 6 2 9 3 8 | 5 1 7 2 6 9 |

**Picture Vocabulary**

1. Airplane_____
2. Telephone_____
3. Hat_____
4. Baseball_____
5. Tree_____
6. Key_____
7. Horse_____
8. Knife_____
9. Jacket_____
10. Boat_____
11. Umbrella_____
12. Foot_____
13. Flagpole_____
14. Cane_____
15. Arm_____
16. Pocket Knife_____
17. Pitcher_____
18. Leaf_____

## Comprehension Questions, Color Forms, Action Agent, and Three-Hole Form Board—Recording Sheet

Name_____

Age_____

**Comprehension Questions:**

A. What must you do if you are:

Hungry?

Sleepy?

Cold?

B. What must you do if you have Lost something?

What must you do when you Cross the Street?

**Color Forms**

**Action Agent**

| | | |
|---|---|---|
| Runs_____ | Cuts_____ | Growls_____ |
| Cries_____ | Blows_____ | Stings_____ |
| Sleeps_____ | Shoots_____ | Gallops_____ |
| Scratches_____ | Melts_____ | Aches_____ |
| Flies_____ | Sails_____ | Explodes_____ |
| Bites_____ | Boils_____ | Roars_____ |
| Swims_____ | Floats_____ | Mews_____ |
| Burns_____ | | |

**Three Hole Formboard**

First Presentation

1. _____  2. _____  3. _____

Rotations

## Identifying Letters & Numbers, Computation—Recording Sheet

Name _____

Age _____

**Identifying Letters and Numbers**

| Name | Point | | Name | Point | | Name | Point |
|------|-------|--|------|-------|--|------|-------|
| A | _____ | | J | _____ | | S | _____ |
| B | _____ | | K | _____ | | T | _____ |
| C | _____ | | L | _____ | | U | _____ |
| D | _____ | | M | _____ | | V | _____ |
| E | _____ | | N | _____ | | W | _____ |
| F | _____ | | O | _____ | | X | _____ |
| G | _____ | | P | _____ | | Y | _____ |
| H | _____ | | Q | _____ | | Z | _____ |
| I | _____ | | R | _____ | | | |

| | | | | |
|--|--|--|--|--|
| 1 | _____ | | 7 | _____ |
| 2 | _____ | | 8 | _____ |
| 3 | _____ | | 9 | _____ |
| 4 | _____ | | 10 | _____ |
| 5 | _____ | | 11 | _____ |
| 6 | _____ | | 12 | _____ |

**Computation**

How high can you count? _____

(If say 100, ask) Any higher? _____

Spontaneous counting _____ (stop at 40)

Calculations: (if you have _____ pennies and I give You _____ more, how many would you have?)

(When completed, say) How did you get it?

$2 + 2 =$        $7 + 3 =$        $14 + 3 =$

$2 + 3 =$        $6 - 4 =$        $16 - 4 =$

$5 - 2 =$

(If unable to calculate, place four pennies two inches apart in a row on the table and say) *Count* them and tell me how many there are.

1 2 3 4

Altogether _____

1 2 3 4 5 6 7 8 9 10

11 12 13

Altogether _____

1 2 3 4 5 6 7 8 9 10

Altogether _____

1 2 3 4 5 6 7 8 9 10 11 12

13 14 15 16 17 18 19 20

Altogether _____

## Motor—Recording Sheet

Name_____

Age_____

| | |
|---|---|
| Pellets | _____ sec. with right<br>_____ sec. with left |
| Walk on tiptoe | Attempts with/without hand held<br>Takes 2-3 steps with/without hand held<br>Takes _____ steps without hand held |
| Skip | On one foot<br>On alternating feet |
| Jump in place | Attempts<br>Both feet leave the floor |
| Jump down | Attempts but steps, or other body parts touch floor<br>Lands on feet<br>Lands on toes |
| Stands on one foot | Attempts with/without hand held<br>Momentary balance<br>Balance of 1-2 seconds<br>Balance of 4-8 seconds<br>Balance of more than 8 seconds |
| Jumps | Standing broad jump |
| Hops on one foot | Hops with both feet off the ground<br>Hops on one foot |
| Beanbag Throw | Throws underhand<br>Throws overhand<br>Advanced throwing (advances—with opposite foot) |
| Beanbag Catch | Attemps but misses<br>Catches with arms against chest<br>Catches with hands against chest<br>Catches with hands alone |

# Appendix C:
# Personal-Social Interview

## INSTRUCTIONS:

The interviewer's job is to ask the questions listed and to indicate the mother's response—where possible, by circling the phrase that best matches it. When uncertain which phrase to circle, write out the response in abbreviated form for later scoring.

Questions within sections are roughly age-ordered; the first question may help to establish overall level. Behaviors obviously long-established (on the basis of the rest of the responses) may be credited without asking; those obviously way ahead of the child need not be asked. But circle one phrase for every question.

The first word or phrase after each question is used when the child has not yet reached the level of behavior described; the last word or phrase when he has reached or gone beyond it. The middle choice, often noted as "qualified," is used when the response is unstable—"it depends," "he tries," "he's learning to," "not too well," etc.

Ordinarily assume ability and preference to go reasonably together. Where the mother separates the two ("He can bathe himself, but he won't do it"), *ask further*. Inquire how often he *has* done so; if he has performed the act five or more times, score as able to do it; if not, score qualified.

Where the question is difficult or interpretation is doubtful, the parent is asked for an example. Record the example the mother gives.

| Child's name | | Date | Age |
|---|---|---|---|
| Informant | Interviewer | | |

| | | | |
|---|---|---|---|
| How well does he manage for himself at meals—does he need much help or just about none? | Needs much | Needs a little | Just about none |
| Does he feed himself without much spilling? | No | Spills some | No spilling |
| Does he use a spoon or a fork to eat? | Spoon | Qualified | Fork |
| How well does he use a knife for spreading? | Unable | Fair job | Spreads well |
| Does he use a knife for cutting things such as soft meats? | Unable | Fair job | Cuts well |
| Between meals, can he get himself a drink without help? | No | Qualified | Yes |
| Can he pour from the milk container without spilling? | No | Qualified | Yes |
| How does he manage at dressing and undressing? | No | Qualified | Yes |
| Can he take off his own pants or slacks? | No | Qualified | Yes |
| T-shirt or sweater? | No | Qualified | Yes |
| Can he put on his own coat or jacket (ignore fastening)? | No | Qualified | Yes |
| T-shirt or sweater? | No | Qualified | Yes |
| Can he unbutton most buttons in front (except under chin)? | No | Qualified | Yes |
| Can he button most buttons in front (except under chin)? | No | Qualified | Yes |
| How about shoes: | | | |
| Can he put them on correctly? | No | Qualified | Yes |
| Can he lace them? | No | Qualified | Yes |
| Can he tie the knot part (*not* the bow)? | No | Qualified | Yes |
| Can he tie them with a bow? | No | Qualified | Yes |
| Can he do a pretty good job of washing and drying his hands? | Poor | Qualified | Competent |

| | | | |
|---|---|---|---|
| Can he wash his face without soaking his shirt? | No | Qualified | Competent |

| How much help does he need to take a bath? | Needs full supervision | Needs some help | Needs touching up | Cares for self fully |
|---|---|---|---|---|

| | | | |
|---|---|---|---|
| Can he put himself to bed without any help? | No | Qualified | Yes |
| Does he ever have daytime accidents, wetting himself? | Sometimes | Rarely | Never |

| Must you remind him to go or does he ask or just go by himself? (What if you didn't remind him?) | Needs reminder | Gets reminder, may not need it | Asks, or cares for himself |
|---|---|---|---|

How much help does he need when he has a bowel movement?
Needs help with clothing and wiping
Manages clothing, needs wiping
Cares for self completely

| | | | | |
|---|---|---|---|---|
| Does he ever have accidents at night (if you don't pick him up)? | Often | Occasionally | Rarely | Never |
| Does taking him up at night help? | No help | Sometimes | Usually | Not needed |

| | | | |
|---|---|---|---|
| Does he ever do little jobs around the house along with you—dusting and things like that? | No | Qualified | Yes |
| Can he set the table? | No | Tries | Adequately |

Can he be outdoors alone? How far from home can he go by himself? How often do you have to check on him?
Always someone with him outdoors
In yard alone, if mother occasionally checks
In own yard alone, without checking
Goes around neighborhood, occasional checks
Goes around neighborhood on own

| | | | |
|---|---|---|---|
| Could you send him to the store? | No | Qualified | Yes |
| Can he be trusted with money—not to lose it—or doesn't he have much understanding of it yet (whether or not he knows specific values)? | No idea of value | Some idea | Can be trusted |

| | | | |
|---|---|---|---|
| Does he understand that different coins are worth different amounts, and that some buy more than others? | No idea | Some idea | Good idea |
| Does he have any idea about what some things cost (under $1)—like a candy bar or toy car? | No idea | Some idea | Good idea |
| Can he tell time at all? No | To nearest hour | To nearest quarter hour | Fairly accurately |
| When he's talking to you, what name does he call himself? | Own name | Me | I |
| Does he ever tell you about things that happened when you weren't there (little stories about school, etc.)? | No | Qualified | Yes |
| Does he ask "Why?" questions, such as "Why is it broken?" *Give me an example* of one you remember. | No | Occasionally | Often |
| Does he ask "How?" questions, such as "How do you do that?" *Give me an example* of one you remember. | No | Occasionally | Often |
| Does he play games in which he imitates things grownups do? *Give me an example.* | No | Briefly, occasionally | Sustained imagination |
| When he's with other children, do they really play together and tell each other what to do next, or does he mainly enjoy being with them and doing the same things? | Parallel play | Mixed | Cooperative play |
| Does he play games such as tag or hide-and-seek, or doesn't he quite get the idea of being *It* and winning or losing? (Don't count just chasing or being chased.) | Does not play | Plays with coaching | Plays with understanding |
| Does he get the idea of taking turns? | No | Qualified | Yes |

| | | | |
|---|---|---|---|
| Does he play any table games such as checkers, tic-tac-toe, or Uncle Wiggley? | No | Learning | Yes |
| Does he use a pencil or crayon to make drawings or designs? | No | Qualified | Yes |
| Does he make things by cutting out, pasting, etc.? | No | Qualified | Yes |
| Does he perform for others—recite nursery rhymes, sing, etc.? | No | With help | Yes |

# References

1. Ames, Louise B. *Child Care and Development*. Rev. ed. Philadelphia: Lippincott, 1979.
2. ———. "Predictive Value of Infant Behavior Examinations." In *The Exceptional Infant: The Normal Infant*. Seattle, Washington: Special Child Publications. Vol. I. 1967. pp. 209–39.
3. ———. *Is Your Child in the Wrong Grade?* New York: Modern Learning Press, 1978.
4. Ames, Louise B., and Chase, Joan Ames. *Don't Push Your Preschooler*. New York: Harper & Row, 1976.
5. Ames, Louise B.; Gillespie, Clyde; and Streff, John W. *Stop School Failure*. New York: Harper & Row, 1975.
6. Ames, Louise B., and Ilg, Frances L. *Mosaic Patterns of American Children*. New York: Hoeber/Harper, 1962.
7. ———. "Variant Behavior as Revealed by the Gesell Developmental Examination." *J. Genet. Psychol.* 63 (1943): 273–305.
8. ———. "Every Child in the Right Grade: Behavioral Age Rather Than Age in Years the Best Clue to Correct Grade Placement." *The Instructor* 73 (November 1963): 7 ff.
9. ———. "Sex Differences in Test Performance of Matched Girl and Boy Pairs in the 5- to 9-Year-Old Age Range." *J. Genet. Psychol.* 104 (1964): 24–34.
10. ———. "The Developmental Point of View with Special Reference to Reciprocal Neuromotor Interweaving." *J. Genet. Psychol.* 106 (1964): 195–209.
11. ———. *Your Two Year Old: Terrible or Tender?* New York: Delacorte, 1976.
12. ———. *Your Three Year Old: Friend or Enemy?* New York: Delacorte, 1976.

13. ———. *Your Four Year Old: Wild and Wonderful.* New York: Delacorte, 1976.

14. ———. *Your Five Year Old: Sunny and Serene.* New York: Delacorte, 1979.

15. ———. *Your Six Year Old: Rebellious but Loving.* New York: Delacorte, 1979.

16. Ames, Louise B.; Métraux, Ruth; and Walker, Richard N. *Adolescent Rorschach Responses.* Rev. ed. New York: Brunner/Mazel, 1971.

17. Ames, Louise B.; Métraux, Ruth; Rodell, Janet L.; and Walker, Richard N. *Rorschach Responses in Old Age.* Rev. ed. New York: Brunner/Mazel, 1973.

18. ———. *Child Rorschach Responses.* Rev. ed. New York: Brunner/ Mazel, 1974.

19. Ames, Louise B., and Walker, Richard N. "Prediction of Later Reading Ability from Kindergarten Rorschach and I.Q. Scores." *J. Educ. Psychol.* 55 (1964): 309–13.

20. Austin, John J., and Lafferty, J. Clayton. *Ready or Not? The School Readiness Checklist.* Muskegon, Mich.: Research Concepts, 1963.

21. Braga, Laurie, and Braga, Joseph. *Learning and Growth: A Guide to Child Development.* Englewood Cliffs, N.J.: Prentice-Hall, 1972.

22. Burns, Robert C., and Kaufman, S. Harvard. *Kinetic Family Drawings* (K-F-D). New York: Brunner/Mazel, 1972.

23. ———. *Actions, Styles and Symbols in Kinetic Family Drawings* (K-F-D). New York: Brunner/Mazel, 1970.

24. Carll, Barbara, and Richard, Nancy. *One Piece of the Puzzle. A School Readiness Manual.* Moravia, N.Y.: Athena Publications, 1977.

25. Chase, Joan Ames. "A Study of the Impact of Grade Retention on Primary School Children." *J. Psychology* 70 (1968): 169–77.

26. ———. "Differential Behavior Characteristics of Non-Promoted Children." *Genet. Psychol. Monog.* 86 (1972): 219–77.

27. Cott, Allan. "Megavitamins: The Orthomolecular Approach to Behavior Disorders and Learning Disabilities." *Academic Therapy Quarterly* 7 (1972): 3.

28. Delacato, Carl. *A New Start for the Child with Reading Problems.* New York: McKay, 1974.

29. Feingold, Ben F. *Why Your Child Is Hyperactive.* New York: Random House, 1975.

30. Gesell, Arnold. *Infancy and Human Growth.* New York: Macmillan, 1928.

31. ———. "The Stability of Mental Growth Careers." In *Intelligence: Its Nature and Nurture.* Bloomington, Ill.: The Public School Publishing Co., 1940. pp. 149–60.

32. ———. et al. *The First Five Years of Life.* New York: Harper, 1940.

33. Gesell, Arnold, and Amatruda, Catherine S. *Developmental Diagnosis.* Edited by Hilda Knobloch and Benjamin Pasamanick. Rev. ed. New York: Harper & Row, 1974.

34. Gesell, Arnold, and Ames, Louise B. "The Ontogenetic Organization of Prone Behavior in the Human Infant." *J. Genet. Psychol.* 55 (1940): 247–63.

35. Gesell, Arnold; Ilg, Frances L.; and Ames, Louise B. *Infant and Child in the Culture of Today.* Rev. ed. New York: Harper & Row, 1974.

36. Goodenough, Florence. *The Kuhlman Binet Test of the Preschool Child.* Minneapolis: The University of Minnesota Press, 1928.

37. Gross, Martin. *The Psychological Society.* New York: Random House, 1978.

38. Hallahan, Daniel P., and Kauffman, James. *Introduction to Learning Disabilities.* Englewood Cliffs, N.J.: Prentice-Hall, 1976.

39. Hedges, William D. *At What Age Should Children Enter First Grade: A Comprehensive Review of the Research.* Ann Arbor, Mich.: University Microfilms International, 1977.

40. Hunter, Madeline. "Right-brained Kids in Left-brained Schools." *Today's Education* (November/December, 1976).

41. Ibuka, Masaru. *Kindergarten Is Too Late.* New York: Simon & Schuster, 1978.

42. Ilg, Frances L., and Ames, Louise B. *Child Behavior.* New York: Harper Brothers, 1955.

43. ———. *School Readiness.* New York: Harper & Row, 1972.

44. Ilg, Frances L.; Ames, Louise B.; and Apell, Richard J. "School Readiness As Evaluated by Gesell Developmental, Visual, and Projective Tests. *Genet. Psychol. Monog.* 71 (1965): 61–91.

45. Ilg, Frances L.; Ames, Louise B.; Haines, Jacqueline; and Gillespie, Clyde. *School Readiness.* Rev. ed. New York: Harper & Row, 1978.

46. Jacobson, J. Robert. "A Method of Psychobiologic Evaluation." *Am. J. Psychiatry* 109 (1949): 330–46.

47. Jacobson, J. Robert, and Pratt, Helen Gay. "Psychobiological Dysfunction in Children." *J. Nerv. and Ment. Dis.* 109 (1949): 4.

48. Jensen, Arthur R. *Understanding Readiness: An Occasional Paper.* Urbana, Ill.: ERIC Clearing House in Early Childhood Education, 1969.

49. Kagan, Jerome. *Change and Continuity in Infancy.* New York: Wiley, 1971.
50. Kaufman, Alan J. "Piaget and Gesell: A Psychometric Analysis of Tests Built from their Tasks." *Child Development* 42 (1971): 1341–60.
51. Koppitz, Elizabeth. *The Bender Gestalt Test for Young Children.* New York: Grune & Stratton, 1964.
52. ————. *The Bender Gestalt Test for Young Children. Research and Applications, 1963–1973,* vol 2. New York: Grune & Stratton, 1975.
53. Levinson, Daniel. *Seasons of a Man's Life.* New York: Knopf, 1978.
54. Meyer, George. "Some Relationships Between Rorschach Scores in Kindergarten and Reading in the Primary Grades." *J. Proj. Tech.* 17 (1953): 414–25.
55. Mulrain, John C. "The Effectiveness of a Shortened School Day Program for First Grades: A Follow-up Study." Dissertation, Graduate School, Temple University, 1977.
56. Oakland, Thomas. *Psychological and Educational Assessment of Minority Children.* New York: Brunner/Mazel, 1977.
57. Pitcher, Evelyn G., and Ames, Louise B. *The Guidance Nursery School.* Rev. ed. New York: Harper & Row, 1975.
58. Postman, Neil, and Weingartner, Charles. *The School Book: For People Who Want to Know What All the Hollering Is About.* New York: Delacorte, 1973.
59. Scott, Betty A., and Ames, Louise B. "Improved Academic, Personal and Social Adjustment in Selected Primary School Repeaters." *Elementary School Journal* 69 (1969): 431–39.
60. Sheehy, Gail. *Passages: Predictable Crises of Adult Life.* New York: Dutton, 1976.
61. Silberberg, Norman E., and Silberberg, Margaret. "The Bookless Curriculum: An Educational Alternative." *J. Learning Disabilities* 2 (1969): 302–7.
62. Slosson, Richard L. *Slosson Intelligence Test (SIT).* East Aurora, N.Y.: Slosson Educational Publications, 1963.
63. Smith, Lendon H. *Improving Your Child's Behavior Chemistry.* Englewood Cliffs, N.J.: Prentice-Hall, 1976.
64. Stringer, Lorene A. "Report on a Retention Program." *Elementary School Journal* 60 (1960): 370–75.
65. Walker, Richard N., et al. *Gesell Preschool Norms Revised,* in press.
66. Wechsler, David. *WISC-R: Wechsler Intelligence Scale For Children.* New York: The Psychological Corporation, 1974.
67. Wunderlich, Ray C. *Allergy, Brains and Children Coping.* St. Petersburg, Fla: Johnny Reads Press, 1973.

# Index